ON THE

OVERNIGHT

TRAIN

ALICE FRIMAN

ON THE
OVERNIGHT
TRAIN

*New and Selected
Poems*

LOUISIANA STATE UNIVERSITY PRESS
BATON ROUGE

Published by Louisiana State University Press
lsupress.org

LSU Press Paperback Original

DESIGNER: Michelle A. Neustrom
TYPEFACE: Fournier MT Pro

Cover photograph courtesy iStockPhoto.com /graffoto8.

Cataloging-in-Publication Data are available from the Library of Congress.

ISBN 978-0-8071-8141-6 (pbk.: alk. paper) — ISBN 978-0-8071-8184-3 (pdf) —
ISBN 978-0-8071-8183-6 (epub)

To Bruce

CONTENTS

FROM *Blood Weather* (2019)

INTRODUCTION

The Blessed Curse of a Lightning Overload

Stephen Corey

I can see only two ways to write an adequately truthful introduction to Alice Friman's *On the Overnight Train: New and Selected Poems,* but I fear that both are beyond possibility. The first would comprise a single sentence along the lines of "You have never read nor will ever read another poetry collection that can stop you so often in your emotional and musical tracks." The other option would be an essay-length (or maybe even book-length) encomium touching on as many of the collection's achievements as possible—but that would take away far too much of the time, feeling, and thought you and other readers ought to be giving to Friman's poems themselves.

So, I will to have to settle for the inadequate and implore you to trust me when I say that the quotes and comments I'll give you here are only urgent surface-scratchers meant to cajole—that's "politely insist upon"—your entry into the complex realm of words, thoughts, emotions, images, musics, ideas, and arguments Friman has conjured and offered up to us (and is still vigorously offering as I write this in late 2023) throughout a writing and publishing career spanning six decades.

The crucial American poet and literary critic Randall Jarrell (1914–1965) claimed that a great poet is one who manages during a lifetime of standing out in thunderstorms to be hit by lightning perhaps a half-dozen times. Without trying to attach any specific integers to the number of lines, passages, or complete poems by Friman that will memorably strike readers of this collection, I am absolutely willing to attest that *I* can recall no poetry volume from my own broad reading experiences that has nailed me/stopped me/caught my breath and my ear and my thinking so frequently. As a result, to read *On the Overnight Train* is both exhilarating and exhausting, both comforting and terrifying, and always more than worthwhile.

Consider, as one of the many instances to come in my praise horde here, the brash and lusty assertions of the title poem's speaker as she and her lover travel the same Polish tracks that carried uncountable thousands to their unwarranted deaths during World War II:

> Look, the body wants what it wants
> when it wants it. But I do wish
> we had found the courage to use
> those purpled hours and put them
> to work: defy decorum and undress.
> Peel off, disrobe, strip down to the very
> bones if necessary. Then, sternum to sternum,
> femur to femur, click into place
> for all those who couldn't, wouldn't
> ever again.

And to Jarrell's lightning strikes (and William Carlos Williams's famous wheelbarrow and white chickens) Friman adds, among numerous other poeticas, a midnight walk on a mountain of lava where her narrator finds one definition of her own search—and oh, that "stretch of Stygian black," with its potent use of consonance *and* mythology:

> Two hours it took to cross
> that stretch of Stygian black,
> having no thought but the need
> to prevail, upright. Now I know
> what it means to balance
> a writer's life. Each footfall,
> each stopping point, a fulcrum
> around which the body teeters
> and sways: a high-wire act
> demanding concentration—

the chattering mind delivered up
blank as cardboard with a pinhole,
dependent, in the pit-dark, upon one
thin thread of dazzle coming through.

A crucial, rare-among-poets, and overall important quality of Friman's lifetime of work to date is that its central subjects and emotions have not shifted very much—yet have seemed to be both new and true because her emotion hoard and her word hoard have each and always offered up exactly those two vital qualities but in novel, unanticipated, and thereby striking ways. As you read through *On the Overnight Train,* you will again and again be brought up short, as I have been, by some version of the same question: "How did she come up with *that?*" And as one of my favorite instances, I will stick with another poem, "The Reckoning," that stays with the same central subject—and earned the following two notes I wrote to myself in my reading copy of the manuscript: Who has ever written such a love poem? and Who has ever successfully written such an X-rated and memorable description of "the act"? Knowing you hold the book in your hands as you read these words, I will allow myself this quoted-in-full example from Friman's 1984 collection, *Reporting from Corinth:*

We meet tonight to pass the point of blame
dealt out like a marked deck
sticky from past games and fingers.
We meet in the hole of last week's fire,
scorched grass, scrub. Two bloodhounds
sniffing at the blackened stones.

On a nearby twig, a mantis
mates and mangles in the same clutch.
It is an old confrontation, an ancient fire:
the horse-drawn gift of Greeks
wrapped in the ribboned knot of Helen's legs
the wet slick that licks the scrotal sac
oils the flare and rages.
The pyre of Troy was struck
when the bed of Paris heaved with heat

running fire down the sweet sheets
scenting blood with lavender.

No wonder of it:
The angel sword was struck in Eden.
It roots where it fell, blazing in orchards.
And we, promised by blossoms, run gathering
bushels of cinders, black and still as nuns.

Living long can be ruinous or a gift for a writer's skills and
reputation, with countless factors contributing to the "which-is-it?" for
any individual. Friman's poetry is still kicking ass and breaking hearts as
she steams toward ninety, with—I believe—the key to her continuing
achievement being a complexly composed personality and perspective.
She is terrorized by death at one moment and stomps on its pathetic one-
act show at the next; she is braced to go onward at one moment by the
long looks she has given to the Holocaust in numerous poems throughout
her life, while at other moments the same considerations shatter her. (I
come to "At the Holocaust Museum" and think, "This is, somehow, the
best poem ever written about that horrendous moment in history"—but
then, twenty-five pages later, I come to "The Waiting Room" and say,
"No, *this* is the greatest." Lightning and then lightning again.) Friman
offers up remarkably tender takes on love for children, parents, and lovers,
yet as already briefly noted she is sometimes gung-ho for the erotic-unto-
pornographic. (And who has ever written such a sad, sexy, knowledgeable
poem as "The Squirrel," which involves the title creature, a home
repairman, the speaker's mother, and God?)

Do you remember that body with which I—well, with which Alice
Friman—began my remarks, that body which "wants what it wants /
when it wants it"? Suffer no thoughts that she disregards the body's
Siamese twin, who gets a title *and* its poem's opening words:

The Brain

The brain always knows
where you are. A triumvirate
of eyes, ear canals, tiny nerves

in the joints phones in regularly.
I'm biting my cuticles. Over
and out. Practicing the tuba. Or
guess what I'm doing in bed with
all this flesh? The brain knows.
That's why you can pass
the neurologist's test: clap hands
in the dark. They'll find each other.

Using twenty percent of the body's
blood supply, a billion gray cells
should be good for something—
discovering a cure, unearthing
the great gray owl of wisdom, re-
reading Aristotle's *Ethics,* remembering
where I left my keys—something
other than smug in their aerie
this Tuesday afternoon being clever
when I'm standing at the window
watching the hawk's persistent
shadow, circling.

This brain at the window belongs, of course, to the poem . . . to the poet offering up the poem . . . to the nearly universal notions of poetry that have evolved around the planet . . . and first and finally to the fortunate reader.

And so I turn over *On the Overnight Train* to you. If any introductory line or passage I have offered up does not appeal to you, fear not—and willingly, even happily, gird yourself for the rich alternatives I guarantee you will find.

Postscript

In my second paragraph above, I lauded Alice Friman's work for its "complex realm of words, thoughts, emotions, images, musics, ideas, and arguments"—and for the most part I have tried to let Friman's lines do the work of supporting that claim sans further comments from me. However,

at the risk of dropping in a bit of editorial hubris, I want to praise
something that strikes me as a quietly brilliant element of her "music,"
something I picked up late in my multiple readings of this collection:
her smart here-and-there use of dashes, the result of which can be subtly
but forcefully important. My favorite instance comes in the third of five
stanzas in "Letter to the Children":

> It is the time—the great lying-in of Autumn—
> and I am walking its wards.
> And I remember it was now, late September
> then on into the deep gully of fall—when the hackberry
> groans and the black oak strains in its sockets, the winds
> pushing in the long forest corridors—
> that I too was born and gave birth.

Yes, as Alice Friman knows so fully, and forcefully, and delicately
well, everything matters—each step on the lava, each sound in each line,
each pacing by punctuation, and even the capitalization of *Autumn*
(to make us think of Keats's great ode).

NEW POEMS

Insomnia in Moonlight

Night, and all my dead wake up,
stretch, jostle, meet and greet.
Make a racket. Either they're
entertaining friends or cloning.
In any case, I'm in trouble.

What I really need to hear
is silence. Outside my window,
the moon—my bio-pic in the sky,
my alter-ego—adjusts her shadow,
the same shadow she wraps me in
when I'm too happy, tucking me
in tight to keep me balanced.

The dead have no need for balance.
They're fixed, and like the fixed star
that is the sun, they're free of shadow.

I prefer the moon, starlit, yes,
but changeable, for when she's full
she wears my child face—round,
sunburnt, and pensive. Last spring
I witnessed a total eclipse, the moon
muscling up to blot out the sun.
I rooted for her all the way, knowing
she'd fail. But you have to admire her,
defying the dug-in armies of permanence:
logarithms, penumbras, trajectories,
geometric progressions, the unerasable
dead, and everything else I don't understand.

Of Marriage and the Lunar Eclipse

They stood outside
shivering in their robes
to witness one of the great
silent movies of the world—
that ancient magic trick
played out in CinemaScope
against a black, January sky.

The surrounding trees
dressed in nakedness
stood still. Not one
trembling twig or leaf
to distract their attention.

And because in the dark
color drains to black and white,
the moon's red face, so high
and far away, became the center
of all that mattered. So they stayed,
wrapped in silence and awe,
heads tipped back and waiting.

Sunlit to shattered red
and back, the moon's story
spun itself out. A tale of break
and breach, distance and separation
and a longing for return
as basic as the tides it pulls—
intrinsic as gravity and the heave
of the grave. The narrative of
a rock, pockmarked and scarred
for having watched us so long.

When it was over and the moon
returned to its old job of
brightening, they went inside,
and lying side by side on their bed
stared at the ceiling. They did not
speak. And when they finally
turned to each other and he placed
his hand gently on her cheek,
she wept, but did not know why.

Refraction at Twilight

What did we see
before we knew what we saw,
before the wink of consciousness
put things in perspective, before there
was perspective, when the eye
was new—wet and simple—and the circle
around the crib pulsed with color, pure
and without context?
                    How the world
tipped so generously then, pouring—hot
and straight from the cauldron—
prisms for newborn eyes. Oh, to be able
to see, if but for a second, the blueberry
a blotch, the overhead trees a shimmy of
green, and Mother's face—that first looming
Picasso of shape and shades—offering
comfort and suck.
                    Yes, yes I know,
skin loosens and flesh fails, but look—
the rose still reddens, and evening shadows
purple the walk. There's little time.
That white light at the end of the tunnel
is anxious as a librarian to take back your colors
before stamping your card and checking you out.

On Beauty, White Tie, and the Absolutes

In the first movie I ever saw,
Fred and Ginger danced inside a cloud
of longing. His body, holding her
tight to the music—the lean
length of him, a magic wand
in the swirl of her skirts. And when
the music swelled, opening the floodgates
to the question only bodies can answer,
my three-year-old heart
lifted to breaking, and I knew
that all I'd ever receive from the earth
would never be enough, for here already
in black and white was perfection.

I know, I know.
A Hollywood trick: music, white tie, a dress.
Klieg lights—moonlight in her hair.
The whole ball of wax.

But I was three.
The hammer of my heart knew better.

Plato too knew perfection. He dubbed it
the absolute. Reason itself
insisted it must exist, for how to measure
who is more good than good, if pure good
doesn't live somewhere? somehow? And what
means beautiful or more so, without
that steel-edged ruler, that Greenwich,
that atomic clock ticking off perfection?

Plato must have conceived his philosophy
when he was three. Before the stylus, the scroll,

and Greek homework. Before all the wonder ran out.
For surely he wept when all that grace
of thought and logic came together on the screen
of his mind, as I did, struck immobile
in my seat, in the dark.

The Peach

I stood on a corner eating a peach,
the juice running down my arm.
A corner in Pergos where he left me,
Pergos where I could catch a bus.
What was I supposed to do now
alone, my hands sticky with it
standing on the corner where he
left me a Greek peach, big as a softball,
big as an orange from Spain, but it
wasn't from Spain but from Pergos,
where I could see his red truck
disappear around a corner, not
my corner but farther up the street,
and only later, months later, back
home when the trees were slick
with ice, their topmost branches
shiny as swords stabbing the heart
out of the sky, the earth chilled under
snowdrifts or as we tend to say, *sleeping*.
But I don't know, frozen maybe, numb?

Dumb Apple

It rankled for years, that epithet
shouted at me while running across
the street—screeching brakes
and a blaring horn. Late for class
or defiant against traffic, I don't recall,
but yes, I was indeed a dumb apple—
deserving whatever scolding I got.

Today is the day for resuscitating
old hurts—insults that stick
because they're true, defacing
like a birthmark or scar, never
to be erased. I was seventeen.
Since that day, decades have passed,
yet the shame of that rebuke still
sticks in my craw like the poisoned
apple stuck in the throat of Snow White,
with no prince's kiss to jolt it loose.

* * *

Reader, will you stick with me,
not turn the page if, from the high
hill of my age, I try a little self-love
for a change, a bit of forgiveness,
and begin again?

* * *

A is for Apple. The first temptation.
Eve's munch. Adam's fall. The judgment
of Paris, and Agamemnon's blood running
rivers of Empire and Roman Beauties,
Northern Spy, Ida Red, Jonathan,

Winesap, Gala, and Golden Delicious
spilling, filling the rumbling bins of history.

Every apple begins with a blossom.
Who wouldn't forgive Eve that first bite,
or the girl I was—autumn's harvest of juice
and sweetness crossing that street. How could
she help but rush, so in a hurry to begin?

Hygiene

When Miss Garvey preached
about the importance of washing
beneath our breasts, we were barely
fourteen. We of the pert and perky,
the new sproutings of last spring.
We of the rose-tipped sundae.
We of the smart-aleck mouth:
what's this "beneath" business?
There was no beneath. We were up-
standing in duplicate and up to date—
saucy, sassy, and more relevant
than we knew. We were upright,
up-and-coming, immortal as summer,
flushed as the cherry in our cheeks.

The only beneath that counted
was beneath a sweater, pointing
to the endless possibilities of
where we thought we were headed.
When we stood firm in our straps,
weren't we, for the first time, armed
with power? The lure of I-dare-you
under the do-not-touch of delicious?

To Miss Garvey—object of our
ninth-grade derision—I apologize,
for now, now that I've gotten so old,
I have indeed developed an under,
a beneath. Sometimes I hear
her muffled voice lecturing from
my own dark crease where she lives,
hunkered down, grousing like
the troll under the bridge and wagging

her finger in perpetual admonition—
hygiene, hygiene. Oh for the days
before underwire and under performance,
each morning cup tilted fresh and sweet.

Shopping with Descartes

Like a supermarket chicken,
a brain weighs about three pounds,
without feathers of course.
Thoughts, like feathers, weigh
next to nothing—whimsies
of no matter. What's a thought?
A twitch, a little quiver in the jelly
quickened to life by a shock
of electricity before slipping
back into the fold it was born in.

Still, thoughts are important.
If I don't come up with a thought
for three days, my brain morphs
into a daisy stuck in the vase
of my neck. After two weeks
I could generate a bouquet.

People who think about thoughts
are philosophers. People who
think about thinking about
thoughts are epistemologists.
The book says God once had
a thought which he tucked inside
a word, which makes God a linguist.
It must have been a big word—
an abracadabra word, powerful enough
to create the sun, moon, earth, lions,
tigers, birds and bugs. Imagine,
all in six days. On the seventh day
he rested—so tired from repeating
his word he had to go to bed without
another thought in his head. And that's
how we got the flowers.

The Reenactment

Each spring the phoebe
returns to lay four eggs.
Our itinerant snake
returns too.

Somewhere under our deck
or invisible on an overhanging
branch, he waits. Coiled in a royal
patience, he waits. He waits through
the laying, through the interminable
sitting, the cracking open, the first
peep, the feeding. He waits.
Nothing moves but his tongue
testing the air until he tastes on some
passing stream of ether

that fledging has begun—that frantic
teetering at nest edge to practice flapping.
To toughen up. Fortuitous too
is Mama's best eater, too big now
tó tolerate four to a bed. (Darwin's dictum
and all.) Time to take over.

When the runt falls—a bit of fluff
pushed out by a brother—the slithering one
unwinds, and before I can get a broom
to sweep him off and away

he has disappeared
with his prize.

How prophetic of him
to wait until sibling rivalry

kicks in. No wonder of it.
Think of all he knew before
he stuffed his shadow into an apple
and offered it to Eve.

Reluctant Image

Winter rain, four days straight.
Rivers rising, trees
loosening their root-hold,
and the sky—despite its wash
and rinse—dirty as a vacuum
clogged with dust. Outside my window
is February undressed—naked trees,
naked ground, and the last leaves
of the white oak trembling in cold.
What the scene needs now
is a child, inside, playing on a rug.
But I don't have one anymore.

How faded and far away
the years of my motherhood.

Besides, the child I envision at my feet
comes from an older time. A child
of inner space and private intricacies,
who instinctively knew how
in a stormy house to create in herself
a hidey-hole, a refuge, an eye to crawl into.

Only when she permits do I see her—
a sudden glimpse at the tail end
of a dream, swish of blue pinafore,
white sandals running away and gone
through the sealed-shut door of waking.
Or once, down a country road,
black-eyed Susans winking from a ditch,
and she not turning when I called.

So I know. If she were at my feet now,
here in winter's last, dark days,
and I tried to lift her to my lap—

if only for affection's sake—she'd
squirm down and away, leaving me
to wonder, what mystery *is* this child
who never comes when my emptiness
needs her most to fill a scene or take
her place in my album—this look-alike,
this other possibility, this lost chance?

The George Washington Bridge

The most beautiful bridge in the world
        —Le Corbusier

That bridge was *my* bridge,
anchored, like me, in the bedrock of Manhattan—
the granite grip of *I'll never let you go.*

I thought of that bridge last Sunday
while we dozed off an afternoon of love.
How one cold night over sixty years ago,
in fog and rain, I hiked that bridge
in boots and a yellow slicker, singing
at the top of my lungs. Yes, I did—
happy being such a singular leap for me.
When, suddenly, I noticed a patrol car
inching along, following me. Two
beefy cops, tough with blotchy faces,
calling to me sweet and gentle-like,
singsong-like, because they thought,
they thought . . .

How could I have possibly imagined
then what they thought, held as I was
in suspension above the roiling Hudson
racing beneath me? I only knew I felt
I had swallowed a star. Before me,
a sweep of lights lifted out of the fog
as if hooked to a heaven, and the red
and white beams of traffic crisscrossing
between New York and New Jersey
streamed streaks of spark and glitter,
turning the rain into lit confetti—just
for me, the happy hub of all that shining.

When they asked what I was doing there,
alone in midnight and wet, I laughed.

Last Sunday, in your arms, lying skin to skin,
how I wished I could dig up that ancient
yellow slicker if only to reclaim the mantle
of my foolishness. Not oblivion so much
as a purposeful forgetting, haunted as I am now
by the shuddering tremble of concrete and cable
and the cold, black water waiting under everything.

A Walk in the Park

After the hardwoods had
dumped their leaves, the trees
were left to the pines—sentries in
green uniforms watching over their sleep.
The poplars, maples, oaks, so stripped-
down naked, you couldn't tell them
from the dead they stood among—
silhouettes cutting their limbs into the sky.
When suddenly, an old lady who walked
among them went down, flat on her face
like a fallen log.

The ambulance crew called her *Lucky*
but that was later, after the hammering
electric shocks and the careening
to the hospital where they stood
shyly in the ER to marvel at her—blinking,
up and awake—whose clothes they had
just cut down the middle to get at her chest.
Here she was, breathing and alive after
they had labeled her code blue, flatlined, gone.

Later at home, when she dreamed of them
in her troubled sleep—watched over
by a monitor with a green eye—they were
mere boys, more at home on the soccer fields
than doing life-and-death work
in an ambulance. Boys, who stopped
their play to watch her walking in the park
as if her life weren't used up already, as if
she still mattered. Then, because they called her
Lucky and they were only players in a dream,
they gathered close, and pelted her with flowers.

On the Overnight Train

I remember an open window, my hair
blown apart by a hot wind, and me
itching to make love. We were headed
east through Poland on the old cattle-car,
tracks glinting like teeth in the moonlight,
and there I was acting like a fifteen-
year-old boy, sexed up and oblivious.
The train hurtled through the dark,
shaking side to side past sleeping towns
where once in a while a spotlight from
a passing depot lit up our silhouette.
You were leery, the windows not
dirty enough to hide us, and me,
playing Alice down the rabbit hole,
Let's see where this path goes, tugging
at your belt and laughing, wanting nothing
but skin between us. That was the night
of repeated visits: passport control
banging on the door, guns drawn,
checking papers, or so they said. Thugs
headed by a dead-eyed woman with
bruised lips, a pen, and a black book.

How to explain away that night, my body
operating on its own, divorced from
history: the country surrounding us
and the crimes committed there.
I tell myself it was the wind and balmy
velvet of the dark or the little green pills
the doctor gave me before we left home,
pills so good you can't get them anymore.

To be honest, there are many things
I'd like to change about my life.
Too much homework never finished,

too many lies to count, too many lovers
and too little love. But that night—
racing through the dark in a rattling
car filled with terror-stricken ghosts
and me, who, but for a trick of fate,
could have been, would have been
among them, one more yellow-starred
child pushed, shoved, jabbed and
jammed in with the whole doomed
lot—is not one of them.

Look, the body wants what it wants
when it wants it. But I do wish
we had found the courage to use
those purpled hours and put them
to work: defy decorum and undress.
Peel off, disrobe, strip down to the very
bones if necessary. Then, sternum to sternum,
femur to femur, click into place
for all those who couldn't, wouldn't
ever again.

True Stories

When I was forty-two
I slung a duffle over my shoulder
and went to Greece alone.

You know what happened.
You read the book, saw the movie.

I opened the door, walked in
and there he was—
Diomedes, Breaker of Horses.
No plumed helmet, no horses.
No wine-dark sea, no sword,
no chariot, but, yes, in the flesh—
stuck at a desk in an office.

I stopped in my tracks.
Athena, koritsi mou, give me that.

You could write this poem yourself.

* * *

But that poem isn't this poem.

This is about 435 Greek men, Jews,
from Corfu. Big men, strong men.
Iron workers, mill workers, construction
workers, dock workers, ditch diggers,
furniture movers. Lifters and haulers.

And how when they were rounded up
and sent to the death camps, they were
singled out for their size and strength
and assigned to be *Sonderkommandos*—
those who under SS whips and clubs

struggled with iron hooks to drag
the dead from the gas chambers,
tear apart the knot of tangled bodies,
yank the gold teeth and feed the flesh
to the ovens. Twenty thousand a day.

This is a story about 435 Greek men
who refused. Which means they were shot,
burned, and up the chimney with everyone else.
If you believe in heaven, they entered clean.
If you don't, well, no good deed goes unpunished.

This is a story about heroes,
and I wonder what my Demetrios—
for that was his real name—Demetrios,
whose muscles strained the seams of his shirt,
whose upper arm I couldn't fit two hands around,
whose black chest hair warmed my neck, my breasts,
who never knew I was Jewish, and if he had
with all his masculinity and Greek pride, what
would he have done? Diomedes, Breaker of Horses.

Pathetic Fallacy

in memory of John Ruskin

The trees outside my window
moan and fling their limbs about,
whipped to a panic by the wind.
They sense the hurricane, eighty
miles east of here prowling the coast,
spreading its news of howl and rain.
Already the sky has darkened
and many a leaf has leapt its twig,
quitting its job of sucking up the sun,
distracted and distraught by what's
coming. And if the agitated stems
twist the remaining leaves to reveal
their undersides, their gray undersides,
what about me this September 29th,
birth date of my son who disappeared,
never to return. Am I not allowed
to read the trees how I see them—
keening for me and all the lost children
of the world? If mine is a case of pathetic
fallacy caused by "inaccurate perception"
or "morbid feeling," as Ruskin said,
I invite him to stand with me here
at my window and feel the glass
tremble under his hand while I fill
him in on today's news: of crashing
and grieving and falling apart, of dread
and rubble and the dead left lying
crooked in the streets. And the trees?
See how they rock in their holes as if
they cannot bear it. Who's to say they're
not beside themselves, bent over double,
struggling to yank out their roots and run away?

Ubiquitous

I speak of suffering. A plight not of the few
but of the many. The artist, wizened

with angst and unappreciated, isn't unique.
You could say the same of a cook dreamily

stirring her pots or a smart-assed lawyer with
a skinny tie and polished mouth. You could

say the same about a thug who splits heads
or an ingenue with red barrettes in her hair.

Take this new virus, decked out like a Christmas
orange, spraying its juice all over the place.

You think it worries, picking and choosing
who to single out, make suffer? Everyone

suffers eventually. The great Russians—
artists all—spoke of purifying the soul

through suffering. But I don't know. Once,
I knew a woman who chose not to suffer

by simply deciding not to give a damn. Not
to care about anyone, anywhere, or anyhow

until the hour came when she'd be declared
beyond caring about anything. That is,

boxed up, a gift to the ground with flowers.
Here she was, a woman who, years prior to

leaving this world, pressed to the window
of her life and, seeing nothing but pain,

traded the years she had left for a one-way
ticket to nowhere, living her last years

a squatter in her own mind. If that wasn't
a kind of suffering, what about those of us

who loved her? Shivering outside in the cold,
stamping our feet, banging on the door?

The Scarf

I didn't want a scarf. I didn't
need a scarf. I just wanted her busy.
There in assisted living—barely
assisted and not really living—
her mind slowly peeling off with
nothing but Bingo and television.
Staring out the window.
                         A project,
a project. Heavy hours require
a project. I talked her into a scarf.
Even with trembling hands and
a ruffled retina she could handle
a task that simple, for wasn't she
queen of yarn and the cable stitch?
Master of wool and bouclé and,
oh, that royal blue dress, knit
when she was still Pierce-Arrow
sleek and beautiful?
                         She chose
purple, had the clerk in the store
cast the stitches. Ninety-one years
she trod upon this earth. My job
for the next five, the final five,
was working to keep her out of it.
Two bouts of pneumonia, broken
bones, a crashed wheelchair,
and the crowning blow, dementia.
Meanwhile, I played cheerleader
for a scarf, overjoyed with over-
seeing how it grew: gluttonous
as a boa constrictor fed on the
purple it was made of. A royal
lengthening to lengthen the little
time she had left.
                         Now, whenever

I wear it, I have to wrap it twice
around my throat, then fling the ends
back over both shoulders, wrestling
it into a double knot. A thirty-footer
with twelve inches of fringe, con-
ceived as a hoax to prove that what
one loves can live forever the way
it was. Like Penelope at her loom,
she kept those needles going so I
could keep *her* going. Trouble was,
there were no suitors to distract her
and no hero-hope of rescue. No one
but me, inheritor of this squeeze,
this chokehold wound around my neck.

Mother's Secret

Hesitating between embarrassment
and defiance, she told me
but not his name. *No good, he was.*
A real womanizer, which meant
in Mother-speak, a liar, although he came
to the house once, desperate to see her.
A man in love and she not letting him in.

A doctor, a rheumatologist
who in examining her swollen fingers,
her aching hands, held them too long,
too endearingly long, then—
patients cancelled, a leather couch—
reached for the pins holding
back her hair, that wild, chestnut fall.

That's all I know. A mystery man
whose name she clamped her lips on
into a hard 93-year-old line. Or did she
forget—she forgot so many things
back then—or just didn't want to say,
not willing to open that door. Until—
softly softly—*Pierre, yes, Pierre.*

I sat, white-knuckled in that vinyl
nursing-home chair, waiting for more.
When suddenly she blinked as if
coming out of a trance, and I swear
I heard a door click shut in her brain,
making that the end of it.

And I want to go on record to say
this poem exists to celebrate "good."
Good for Pierre the rheumatologist
who gave her a gift on a leather couch:

a glimpse into the raw center of herself
she never knew. Good for the babysitter
she hired for three-year-old me so a little
tenderness could happen. Good for my father,
Mister "slam-bam thank you ma'am," who
never found out. And good for the trees
sashaying outside my window as I write this,
slapping their leaves together in applause.

Weighing In

What makes these corpses so damn heavy?
      —Dostoevsky

Even the great Russian
wondered what makes dead bodies
so leaden it takes six musclemen
to heft one box. You'd think
life having left would make flesh
less dense, the way a November leaf
floats, skips, and scrapes along a cracked
sidewalk, weightless without its juice.

Of course there's the custom
of adding weight. A coin placed
on the dead one's tongue for fare
across the Acheron or two gold
pieces on eyelids to insure sight
in the underworld. Consider Tut,
the boy king, whose tomb groaned
with groceries, games, a golden
hippopotamus, and a favorite chair,
plus four canopic jars holding
the royal innards. Now, that's heavy.

Not taking chances and wanting
him prepared, I pressed a coin
in my father's hand for carfare.
It must have been a 1935 nickel,
a buffalo nickel, making his box
so heavy. A hoof-kicking, two-ton
heave and shudder bellowing against
the sides, there where I laid my head
to say goodbye before the workmen

engaged the winches and lowered
him, inch by swaying inch, down.

Mother came equipped with her
own added weight. At the moment
of death, she clenched her teeth,
locked her jaws, and sucked in hard.
No last words, no rattle. Just that
hissing intake of breath, never
to be released. What was it
she dared to grab from the air
like a starving person a crust
to keep forever? What spring?
What blackberry summer?
All I know is, in her high hour
she yanked the umbilical chain
and took a piece of me with her.

Sun Struck

I'm sitting in the armchair by the window
trying to write the great American poem
when the sun starts nuzzling my neck and
dropping his best shine over my shoulder
to light my paper and pen as if he gives
a pffft for literature, let alone my poetry.
For eight days now he's been missing.
Once he took up with a little London fog
because he heard some song on the radio.
And now again.
                    So here he is, trying to
apologize, sending flares, flashing his
sunspots. If I didn't know better I'd say
he feels guilty, letting the storm clouds
have their way—drowning newly fallen
leaves, leaving pastures soggy and sullen
with wet—then taking off again without
notice from his old maintenance job of
drying things up. He complains he's not
an appliance and resents being compared
to a dryer in a laundromat. And now, see—
here he is, big baby, trying to make up,
plastering his silly, smiley face all over
my windows, begging. My friends say
I should leave, but truth tell, I love him.
I really do, even when I get sore and rev
things up, especially when he points out
what a big star he is, not just a movie star
like Bogart or Valentino but the real thing.
I tell him to quit whining and remind him
how he's no Extra Large, just an ordinary
Medium stuck in a suburb of an average
galaxy, and if that's the hottest argument

he can muster, forget it. I pull the shades.
Let him cool his heels. But I bet he feels
bad. When I peek, I see him working up
a sweat: splitting atoms, burning hydrogen,
boiling off the helium, counting his mega-
watts, adjusting his $E=mc^2$, all the while
reining in eight planets and shooting off
his rays.

      I know, to forgive may not mean
entirely forget, but when I think of all he
does for me—waxing the moon, making
daisies grow—and how he puckers up to
say good night, leaving a purple and gold
smear of himself out my window, a sort
of kiss which is the one poem he's able
to write, I remember that when I *do* leave,
because one day I will have had enough,
he'll still be around, just you wait and see,
showing the world how much he loved me.

Reporting from
Corinth

(1984)

Economics

Every year the peacock drops his tail,
rains down glory from the fence post,
flinging his wealth away.
                         The trees too
hold their leaves, wait for payday
then dump gold.
A cardinal feeds among sparrows.
The sun shines down on everything.

In Italy where walls tilt with treasure,
Keats lies narrow in his bones,
his only wealth, the two coins
slipped from his shrunken eyes.
Yet people come, in jeans and backpacks,
in pleated voile and Gucci shoes.
Blue-haired ladies and gentle men,
up the Spanish steps to see
where one who spent himself
had lived.
               In my backyard, the lesson repeats.
It is July, the season of gathering up,
the plumping before the harvest.
The accumulation of funds.

What is your life
if all you've done is weed an empty patch of dirt?

Don't ask the trees.
They're busy pulling water,
    pushing out the leaves.

The Reckoning

We meet tonight to pass the point of blame
dealt out like a marked deck
sticky from past games and fingers.
We meet in the hole of last week's fire,
scorched grass, scrub. Two bloodhounds
sniffing at the blackened stones.

On a nearby twig, a mantis
mates and mangles in the same clutch.
It is an old confrontation, an ancient fire:
the horse-drawn gift of Greeks
wrapped in the ribboned knot of Helen's legs
the wet slick that licks the scrotal sac
oils the flare and rages.
The pyre of Troy was struck
when the bed of Paris heaved with heat
running fire down the sweet sheets
scenting blood with lavender.

No wonder of it:
The angel's sword was struck in Eden.
It roots where it fell, blazing in orchards.
And we, promised by blossoms, run gathering
bushels of cinders, black and still as nuns.

Clotho

Clotho sleeps in a bed to die in
so she can dream. A bed of nightmare
and ebony roses, high and dark
as the last hour. She never moves.

Dreams fly under her lids like wild
birds, crying in their brief awakening
before they're gone, still damp and dazed.
Their long legs trailing into the sky.

Once in a thousand years, a man
invisible as the other side of the moon
holds her cupped in his living flesh,
and from under her porcelain lids
she spins one long thread of tears.

Snow White: The Mirror

Even after she left
to follow her necessity—stepping through
her ritual of trial, I held her
in the locket of my frame.

She never spoke of it, but knew,
for she in her child way would stare at me
then slip her long white dress
unbraid the black silk rope of hair
and stand—her budding snow
        fluttering the edges of the dark.

She sought like Psyche to see the face of Love
and I her only candle:

        Mirror, Mirror on the wall
        Who is the fairest of them all?

that I, trembling, brimmed the silver legend
of my heart and gave her back
the sight she gave to me.

Sometimes even now on snow-white nights
when the moon spills her name across the floor
I think I hear her footstep on the stair
and in the silver jelly of my eye
light, so she might see, the votive candle
then float the only constant I have known:

My own white girl. My snow narcissus. Crown.

Snow White: The Prince

She was my perfection once—
An ivory heart
A white bud stopped in stone.
And because she'd never change
I could have filled cathedrals with my love.
My cold virgin. My wafer. My cup.

I did not count on the accident.
Or the children for that matter.
                    Do you hear them?
                    She'll play with them sometimes
                    out in the fields. Her black hair
                    streaked with gray, her waistline
                    gone.
I cannot bear to look.

I like it better here.
This glass from Venice. It's very rare.
And this Egyptian ankh—symbol of life
Frozen in its own silence.
And this quaint piece:
The mirror from the old house. You must have
Heard of it. Go ahead. Study it if you wish.
I can't bear the way it makes me look—
    my eyes too close together
        dark blotches on my skin.
I'll say it needs to be re-silvered, but she won't have it.

She'll come at night sometimes
When she's alone.

I can't imagine what she sees.
Heaven only knows.

Stumbling on Paradise

How much were the stars that night,
Down like lanterns green-swinging,
The moon creaming the water,
Dancing naked in all that shining?
In Kyparissia the sun sets into the
Middle of the sky before it hits the sea,
Tucks like a nickel in a slot
And everyone goes up the hill to
Sip ouzo and watch it drop.
In Kyparissia the apricot tree
Mingles with spearmint and bursts
Golden in the glare of the Greek
Sun streaming off Alekos in the
Red truck going for roast lamb and
Wine and bread, lighting his cigarette,
Drinking the smoke like a thirst.
And only in Kyparissia tastes
Like that, smells like that,
With the sand white and the
Stars rising over his shoulder
And me wrapped to him and
Saying his name, saying his name
Beyond wondering why or how
All the lines could come together like that.
Like the arrows in a tulip's throat
Or the needles in a rose quartz eye.

Riding High

at the Museum of Coaches, Lisbon

When Clement Eleventh went to tea
Or other Papal industry
He didn't take the train or bus
Like common ordinary us
But sat in most uncommon state
Resplendent in his coach-and-eight.
Indeed, it's down in Holy Writ
That Papa Clement scored a hit
Each time he went among the masses,
Preferring them to upper classes,
For living poorly in a hovel
Teaches one the art of grovel.
And so they came from miles around
To be amazed and lick the ground.

They say the sight of the coach alone
Was blazing bright as God's own throne,
Studded with jewels and covered with gilt,
Conceived in heaven and custom-built.

On each right angle of the roof
Four cherubim played as if 'twere proof
That angels flew among the horses
Scaring off Satanic forces.
And six jeweled saints from the Holy See
Mingled with gods of mythology,
Thus all manner of belief
Protected the coach in bas-relief:
St. Francis guarded locks and catches,
Aphrodite watched the latches—
Thus sex and sainthood strangely mingles
Causing chaste off-color tingles.
Athena too in Olympic splendor

45

Brandished her sword above a fender,
And even a lion or two made sure
His Holiness was kept secure
Or made to feel that by and large
Surrounded by that entourage,
Papa Clement would think it right—
Indeed, quite proper in God's sight—
If a beggar whose only thought was bread
Were struck by the coach and left for dead,
To trade in his life for a heavenly copy,
Being bashed in the head by the Pope's jalopy.

FROM

Inverted Fire

(1997)

Stars

Heraclitus said
stars are bowls of inverted fire.
In Delos, yes, where they hang from ropes
or Kyparissia, holding up the soft-backed black
like buttons in a love seat. Here
the world's infection makes them dim.

I remember a Greek night,
counting the spread of stars above my head
plus the two broken in his eyes—
a Peloponnesian beach and me
clinging to him, *Alekos,* saying
Alekos, until the moon rose
bleaching the sky tame. Even I
turned alabaster, while behind him, the waves
hunched and groaned under their fallen cargo—
the gleaming crockery of the drowned.

Now, the sky is filled with ghosts:
ashes in the bottom of their bowls
too deep even for the winds
that prowl down the skies sniffing at rims,
howling for a wildness that burns.

Angel Jewell

I give you the end of a golden string
Only wind it in a ball,
It will lead you in at Heaven's gate
Built in Jerusalem's wall.
　　　　—Blake

Was it the fatal perfection of her name
that sent her among us, so thin
the veins showed in her finger tips?
Skin drawn tight as cellophane
was window on a painting we couldn't bear to see.
Her eyes were blue, too large. Her hair
a cirrus cloud. She lived on air.

What had she to do with what we were—
jostling our corn-fed shoulders, hefting
our packs, our books, our good red laughs?
And of the attentive earth—
the slant barn roof,
the Holstein's swaying bag,
the worm-churned dirt that works the seed,
wraps the root and pushes out the food—
what had she to do with that?
From the beginning she was heaven's freight.

We must have known before she left.
Why didn't we gather then
to press in her pocket as she passed
or in her hand, a note on onionskin
or other weightless thing—the way they stuff
the cracks in Jerusalem's ancient wall
with wailing or a plea?

Love in the Time of Drought

Only at the movies do we slide in,
our elbows on the armrest
then the upper arms
hinging us like the cylinder of a luna moth:
two wings breathless on either side.
You sigh and then an imperceptible groan
as if you were haunted all your life
by this. I look at your face.
You are studying the coming attractions,
afraid there'll be a test.

Look, this summer the only fire
waiting to happen is in the fields, so dry
cows cut their tongues and Queen Anne's lace
swallows down like pride.
Besides, my old insomniac heart
is chained to its army cot. Watch the movie.

It's a story about Rome in a wet July and
two lovers arm in arm on the Ponte Sant'Angelo
where from the railing Bernini's wind-
whipped angels watch their eyes out blind.
The rain comes down like tears.

I am too old for feeble episodes
in lockstep order. I want what angels miss
in their pale heaven that makes them
come down, ecstatic in drapery, to stand,
hands out and empty, crying in the rain.

Birthday in Autumn

At 4 o'clock
October tips her light
in low through any west window
and a dirty cup holds
in some forgotten sink
a sun spot
to the curve of its tea.

Now more than any other time
should cold and heat weigh each other
out and the balance beam level: the promise
holding its own against the graying hairs.

Yet when October comes
carrying gold in her slotted spoon,
as if she bid me feed on what runs
streaming out, I'm not fast enough
and clamp my teeth on empty metal.

What is the message
but to put aside the shudder
of finality—this dying animal
that has carried me like a crown
through tangled streets, the inevitable
white-haired bone—so the harvest
can pour itself into its baskets,
sheer and gold?

October 20
and once more the wild gift:
ribbons of birds,
a rustle of generosity,
the dancing drift of bread.
I should grow fat on such manna.
But all I see are arms

like half-forgotten selves, stretching
in their raveling blouses, thin and
delicate as a young girl's again,
to take November when he comes
in all his privilege,
in all his icy heat.

Invitation to a Minor Poet

Canadian Rockies

Here 70-foot pines clap short arms
like thalidomide kings
in the chinook winds. Here
the mountains wake in a face-off
with the sun and ride nights
motionless on the horns of Capricorn.
Here elk sniff, snort, threaten
then scratch their rumps
on a tree. Here is
imperial nonchalance—
the snow fields trailing off
Mt. Rundle's rocky back. And I
behind the glass of this safe
window in my stolen sweater—
the one I found and used for need
and kept for gratitude, like Claudius
warmed by the sin he was never sorry for—
wait for the lonely crescendo of each day
as if it were a play within a play
behind museum glass. Squirrels
chut-chut from the branches, waggling
the stubby fingers of the pines,
making invitation into a forgiving world
not that different from my own.
See, they say, the trees on the high
rocky face are like stubble
on a Sunday morning. Like Auden
you too can be at home in this world.

Recovery

Little by little the body comes back,
the functions falling in orderly
as a shuffled deck. There's no pushing.
The body is patient as a rug.
Only the mind whines, circles its spot,
will not lie down. Even the saint,
cool in her whitewashed corner,
wrings her hands over her wound.

I examine the incision in the mirror, worry
the seepage lacing through like confession,
the line of the axe, its dizzy intrusion,
while the body (that old hod carrier)
goes about its business: walls and ramps,
the composition of structure, the blood
factory clicking in the bone.

Of the pale mind's fire—the diabolic
urge of the pen, the abracadabra to record
all snooty sensibilities of shock—the body
requires now only distraction,
as Hercules at the gates threw cakes
to the three-headed dog to still his yammering
when there was rescue to be done.

Flight to Australia

Flying backwards
into the day after tomorrow
I think—this perpetual night—
of the invisible curve
we cling to, each in our ten-seat-across
row, huddled in blankets
balancing the cup
buttering the roll: the curve
that holds us to what matters: schedules,
children, the one in the yellow sweater
who kissed and clutched me goodbye.

The group from Vantage Tours
wear blow-up pillows around their necks,
name tags with stars.
They settle to sleep in tandem
as if they learned how from a manual.
The men from Lennox Furnace
talk of blowers and last year's
week in Rio when sales were high.
They flip the pages of their magazines,
adjust their bellies for the long haul. Their wives
lean back delicately.

In Honolulu where we stop, less
than a third of the way there, we gather
at the bathroom mirror, eye each other
warily under the fluorescent tubes,
brush our teeth, our hair, and try
to make up again the face
behind which we make up the world.

How many dinners can we eat? how many
bad movies can be swallowed down before
we grow fuzzy again, run our tongues

over our teeth, grunt in an alien sleep?
Twenty hours between sunset and rise, the limbs
ache for the old familiar parent, not this
stepmother of discomfort who
straps us to her like guilt. Who was it
buried the dead sitting up in a narrow box?

Outside, the moon stretches back,
grins in her wide black bed.

This unnatural sleep reminds us
of the other, but when *that* comes
who will care enough to mind?
It's life that is uncomfortable,
sets the heart to ache, makes us,
like a ten-month pregnancy,
strain the confines of even good intentions.

Even the members of Vantage Tours
begin to struggle against their straps.
No pillow of comfort
can soften the news outside this cabin window:
The moon has disappeared.
The stars are fixed in disinterest.
And anywhere beneath the distraction of our own noise
a shark wakes and cruises in the corrugated sea.

Snake Hill

to my mother

We are on the final avenue.
Hush now. What's to speak?
Soon we'll go down Snake Hill,
cobblestones and weedy lots.

Will you sing to me as we go?
In the toy store window, the guitar
I wept my heart out for,
the rubber bands still stretched with song.
We can buy it now. There's no end
to what we can afford.
                        I'm lying.
It's gone. The window.
The store. The whole corner where
Frank's Market spilled crates out to the curb.
But I'm still there, wailing,
and you pleading reason to *I want*
I want. (What early prick of glass
keeps that vein open still?)

Snake Hill is steep.
The lyrics overflow the hour. After,
it will take me years to turn
and face that climb alone,
each paving stone weed-wet with song
catching at my throat, my throat
filled with you.
                    Only the child
at the top of the hill
can yank me up again—by the heart's cord

running down the roof of her mouth
to the cut bands of the throat—the child
who has no other choice, having nothing left
from that corner to retrieve.

On Loving a Younger Man

One day when I am 91
you will look at me from the doorway, leaning
with your head tilted to one side,
and I will wonder if you remember
how I used to lean
and lay my hair down black and whispering
on the pillowcase fresh from the wash, or how
later I would turn
tucking my knees under yours
for the night's insensible hours.
    And if I haven't forgotten—my mind
gone blank as a sheet—I'll remind you then
of the old amazed look your face wore once
at how much your hands already knew,
and I will call you back
from the doorway
to adjust the sweater around my shoulders,
the robe in my lap, and take your hand, upturned
in mine, to show you how that line is still there:
the lifeline I once traced with my nail,
that day on the bench by the Ohio River, that first
time, when I—troubled—leaned my head on your shoulder,
sideways, the way I do now
and you will then.

Letter to the Children

In the new cold of late September
the prongs of Queen Anne's lace that held
their doilies up like jewels
rise then stiffen, crushing toward center,
making wooden enclosures to die in
like the ones the Celts built to hold their enemies
then set aflame. The goldenrod leans,
licks at their cages. And all that's left of daisies
are burnt-out eyes.

I walk these back fields
past the swish of cattails in their silver
grasses, the old ones
showing the woolly lining of their suede jackets,
while the thistle, dried to gray,
bends her trembling head
and spills her seed.

It is the time—the great lying-in of Autumn—
and I am walking its wards.
And I remember it was now, late September
then on into the deep gully of fall—when the hackberry
groans and the black oak strains in its sockets, the winds
pushing in the long forest corridors—
that I too was born and gave birth.

And you are all Autumn's children, all
given to sadness amid great stirrings,
for you were rocked to sleep in the knowledge
of loss and saw in the reflection outside your window,
beyond the bars of your reach, your own face
beckoning from the burning promise
that little by little disappeared. What can I give you
for your birthdays this year, you who are the match

and the flaming jewel, whose birthright consumes itself
in the face of your desire?

If you were here with me now
walking down this day's death,
I would try to show you two things: how the last light
plays itself out over the thistle's labors,
over the wild cherry heavy with fruit, as if comfort
lay in what it had made. And how that black bird
with flame at his shoulders
teeters for balance on a swaying weed.

Night Drive

Tonight the trees are tossing the clouds around
and the moon in her wedge of white make-up
leans back to hold us in her spotlight of hair.
A dog barks. A garage door lowers and locks.
And every building freezes for the portrait of the world.

Where is defeat on such a night as this?
Each pebble on the side of the road
shouts a victory in the flash of my headlights,
for I have come to the end of fifty-five years,
each one the eraser for the last, each one
a newly sharpened pencil jabbing me awake
to this picture—here and hung—on this night's black wall.

And I am driving, driving for Jimmy Wonderland
down the white line of my own intentions,
glancing in the rearview mirror with a stone's cold eye.
And I know I have never been here before
for I've thrown the old key out the car window to lie
in a ditch somewhere in a broken spill of trash—crockery,
eggshells, an unloved dolly clutching at the dirt.

Imagine what you like: say this film
is a loop played round and before, or that I drive
a winding hill passing the same sign on repeated rights.
But it is night. The dark surrounds, presses, then
slides off. I *see* no sign but this white immediacy
quickening in the brights of my car. And nowhere
beyond the reach of my eyes is more sweet than here
when marrow blooms in the bone and starts to speak.

FROM *Zoo*

(1999)

In Medias Res

In a lawn chair under a tree
Eve woke. Those golden
delicious—three on a stem,
patient as pawnbroker balls—
clinked in the always May.

A pangolin uncurled at her feet.
An elephant lowered his pizzle
to start Lake Victoria.
It was the seventh day.
Eve rested. Across her lap
a shadow. Raven—
stitching a black thread
into the sky. Eve touched
her left breast, a meandering
vein twisting around her nipple
like a hook.

Even before the Greeks,
four lions, abracadabra
on a ledge, blinking, heavy
in the sun. A zebra carcass
twenty feet away, already eaten.

Vultures

Masai Mara, Kenya

Iron beaks to a magnet, they come.
Circle once, twice, then settle. Spread
their wings into a tablecloth of frenzy,
heads ducked under to feed.
And when they're done, zebra ribs stick up
like fence palings of an abandoned house, all black-
white curtains of decency shoved aside.

But when zebra fall, sick or old, not
run down by cheetah or lion ambush,
but intact, the striped wall impregnable,
it's not what you imagine.

They start with the eye, the one staring up.
One snake-necked Whiteback teeters on the head
then, steady, dips into the socket.
The bird's head, single-minded as a straw,
enters easy, neck down in a bone collar. Retina,
macula, up the optic jelly to the zebra's whole
brain box of pictures. God, the hunger
to feed a crop, to suck out the cones and rods
of grasses, the horizon's steady pull, to bulge
remarkable with another's stash.

On the other end, the great rump,
stilled from twitching flies, lies open as a road map.
Tail fallen aside. Stripes to the right,
the left, pointing the way.
A vulture's head moves in, the beak
careful and deliberate as an oiled glove.

The Samburu say vultures dream
the location of food. Maybe in a dream
you too saw—a ravine, black buffalo
lion-gutted, hyena pacing—and suddenly
stood stunned to watch the hide
fill and shimmy alive again. Not with maggot
or crawly thing, but something bigger. Mother
of nightmare, of hissings and black rags.
Mother of crucibles, Nekhebet
the vulture-headed, draggled with wings.

Honeymoon

Ngorongoro, Tanzania

When lions mate they disappear for days,
come together six, eight times a morning.
We saw them on the ridge, he swaying over her,
she on her back fondling his ears, his mouth.
I swear she raked the mane back from his face
and he, intent on nothing but her yellow eye.
Later they'll hunt, feed muzzle to muzzle
snarling in the kill, then lick each other clean
to hold on the tongue the blood taste
from the beloved's face. Such petting.
Such lion love. The sky arching above them—
vast Ouranos heaving himself on top of Earth,
his old girl, glancing over his shoulder
with his bluest eye to copy what he had begun.

The Squirrel

Her fame lasted a week, the running
tale of the neighborhood. Even after
the man from Central Heating and Air came,
gagged into his handkerchief, while I
steadied the flashlight, held the plastic bag.

We never knew how she got in,
but we knew her terror—knocked over plants,
broken glass, a spew of droppings on the stair.
Our neighbor said he'd seen her peering out
our windows like an orphan through a fence.
We tried everything, back door ajar,
acorns across the threshold, but by then
we'd heard nothing for days, so we knew.

He had to unscrew bolts, the furnace doors,
pry open a fist of wire to get her out.
In the whole world of the basement
why did she ram herself into a space
no wider than an inch? A corridor to nowhere.
Between two walls. Upside down, swollen and stuck.

The repairman turned away.

Close the curtains. Wrap us in hymns.
Twist in our hands something beautiful,
then burn, bury it, but God, don't open it.
Flesh, sorry flesh, the dirt that dampens,
that smells. Our little fat
jammed between the two walls of nothing
that closes in when life doesn't want us
and there's no more room.

On the underside of animals, there is
what feels like a seam. In the privacy

of your hand, you know this.
Vertical along the scrotum, then forward
or back. In women, the short line
between gaps. What did Mother call it?
The baker's pinch to seal shut the dough?
A *bon voyage* from the slip of God's mouth?

The squirrel was pressed head down in a steel suit
with no air or room to scratch the sound
that might have saved her.
And when the furnaceman undid the sides
and she slid, heavy into the black plastic,
the body turned and I could see,
all along her belly's length, a faint line.
The darker hairs on either side combing together
the way gears mesh and lock, the way a zipper closes.

Hunger

All love has the tug of the first nipple.
Go to Rome. Romulus and Remus
still patty-cake in the shade of a hairy teat
even in public. Soon typewriters will be obsolete
but never that. It's the gold chain
back to the breast pocket, love's first taste
without the sting of salt: rosebud fresh
and wet in the mouth.

The Hawaiians used to say
spirits leave the body through the inner angle
of the eye and return through the feet,
struggling up the body's dark passages.
But I say, love—the singing *Ahhhh*
every tongue depressor's looking for—
makes a home inside the mouth and stays there.
That's why at birth the mouth is readied,
swabbed clean as a foyer. What else
is man's facial hair but welcome mat for more?
A broom sweeping up around love's entrance.

Even at the end, under oxygen,
eyes shut, fingers no more than dried leaves
whispering to the sheets, the mouth
sucking, sucking on the exhausted tongue.

The Longing

Puna Coast, Hawaii

I never walked at night
   but once. The moon full.
      The sea jacked crazy. And I

hanging on the one scrub palm
   at cliff's edge watching the moon
      focus her telescope, her pet

beast crawling in on watery knees
   then rising against the lava cliffs
      only to crash and fall back

seething in a white blood
   then gather itself up
      like mercury home to its drop

to do it again. I tell you
   I raised my arm
      making of my hand an eclipse

to stop it, cap the moon
   like a Mason jar, gag of wax
      and a rubber ring. Might as well

string a hair across the road
   to trip motorcycles—this trying
      to skid the wheels, hold one idea

high and steady in your mind,
   diamond hard and
      patient as that palm.

Under Water

There is no bottom
to the bottom of this world.
The wind grieves oceanic. And limbs
of the sixty-foot spruce darkening my window
grope restless as eelgrass or the swaying
tentacles of Salome, liquid in her veils.
You know that story. John the waterboy
lost his head to her. And she,
stuck forever in the dance—two feet
jammed into one shoe.
Punishment enough for anybody.

Imagine each year of your life
like that. A fever of telephone poles.
A string of paper dolls. Of showgirls
wearing two dimes and a nickel, imitating
columns screwed into the stairs.
Even the Rockettes, New York's row of hearts—
pistons for knees, jumpy as jackhammers,
kicking in place to no place at all.

Days like this I understand
why women are pulled to water, walk the beach
watching like Easter Island mysteries
as if the sea were a melt of crystal ball
or a lady's mirror leaky with yearning.

A wise woman covers her mirrors.
What sign can be hoped for?
The moon walks pulling a silver leash,
and the old sea, that mother, that bitch
long in the tooth and foaming in her collar, heels.

Storage

Earth is the planet of storage.
Any hollow will do. The Hawaiians said
an anguished soul flutters about the body
until scooped up and stoppered in a gourd.
Drags at is more like it. On the day
we decided to put Daddy in the home
he fell three times. His legs, disobedient
as a bundle of sticks. On his knees
facing the chair he fell out of, the seat
chest-high and inaccessible as his mama's lap
gone these thirty years.

I squatted behind him—we who don't speak,
hadn't touched for fifty years—shins
at his back for leverage, arms around his chest,
locked at the wrists, tugging at dead weight.
Under my pulse, the galley-drum of his heart
banging orders to the rubbery legs, swishing
like so much flotsam on the carpet.

How many times a day do you call 911?

He clawed at the chair's arms, his diaper
slipping off his crack. *Lift me*
he roared. His bald head, face down,
burrowing in the back seam of the chair
as if the fontanel had opened again
and somewhere in that cushion's softness
winked the old keyhole—the wet slit out.

How many times a day? How many an hour?
Now each night I fall asleep like a fish—
eyes open, afraid to close them.
So small. His belongings—
two suitcases next to a strange bed.

Diapers for My Father

Pads or pull-ons—*that*
is the question. Whether to buy
pads dangled from straps
fastened with buttons or Velcro—
pads rising like a bully's cup
stiff as pommel with stickum backs
to stick in briefs. Or, dear God,
the whole thing rubberized,
size 38 in apple green, with
or without elastic leg. Or the kind,
I swear, with an inside pocket
to tuck a penis in—little resume
in a folder. Old mole, weeping
his one eye out at the tunnel's end.

The clerk is nothing but patience
practiced with sympathy.
Her eyes soak up everything.
In ten minutes she's my cotton batting,
my triple panel, triple shield—my Depends
against the hour of the mop: skeleton
with a sponge mouth dry as a grinning brick
waiting in the closet.

She carries my choices to the register,
sighing the floor with each step.
I follow, absorbed away to nothing.

How could Hamlet know what flesh is heir to?
Ask Claudius, panicky in his theft,
hiding in the garden where it all began
or behind the arras, stuffing furbelows
from Gertrude's old court dress into his codpiece.
Or better, ask Ophelia, daughter too

of a foolish, mean-mouthed father,
who launched herself like a boat of blotters
only to be pulled babbling under the runaway stream.

The Book
of the Rotten
Daughter

(2006)

The Dream of the Rotten Daughter

On the night of the day
she buried her mother

her father turned to her
from the grip of an old

photograph, her six-year
dead daddy, swiveled his

bullet head, nailing her
to him with a bloodshot

sniggery eye, then stuck
out his tongue. She woke up

laughing, recognizing
the title of this poem

before she wrote it, there
on the point of that red

wad where he'd honed it all
those years, slipping it in

between her ribs when she
least expected. It was

his label for her from
the time of the big bed

Sunday mornings, and she
between them pretending

oblivion, a balled-
up cuddle to bridge their

unbridgeable gap. Or
(speak truth, oh rotten one)

usurp the I'm-here-first
of that furious eye.

Old news, old news. Tell it
another way. Make it

a Halloween story,
Poe story—ghouls, spiders,

cellars and foul air. Two
dolls in their boxes, laid

side by side like people
bewitched in an iron sleep

and a ghost with a blood
eye and a butcher's tongue

who cut his way into
his daughter's dream to say

of the newly dead, *Boo!*
I won. I've got her now.

After Shooting the Barbados Ram

Because his neighbor's boy wanted the horns
he whacked off the top of the head
straight across
leaving the brain in the grass—
two tablespoons of squiggle
and the brain pan
lined in ivory, empty except for the flies.

I watch because I must,
not because my grinning brother-in-law
waving his bloody knife
shoves the scene in my face—the ram
strung up by the hind legs
then slit down the middle, the insides
tumbling out into a tub. The one
undescended testicle, knuckle big
and hard as love,
flushed from its hiding place at last.
The body, the hide, adding up to nothing
but a magician's coat emptied of its tricks.
Any two-bit fly buzzy in emerald
is more than this.

But it's the brain I come back to,
separated from the white fibrous fingers
that cradled it, suspended it
easy in a jelly. The Dura Mater.
The enduring mother, holding—
idiot or saint—whatever she's got.
Mama the dependable, tough as bungee straps
or a stevedore's net, hanging on
to her freight until the final dock.

I kneel in the grass,
run my fingers over the brain's empty casing,

think of my father, gone not even a month.
A meningioma, they said. A thickening
of the outer lining. The Dura Mater.
The tough mother who never quits,
who quit. Took up weaving in her boredom,
knitting her own cells into a pile of pillows
then turned, the way milk turns,
the way any mother left alone in the dark
might turn, a pillow in her hands.

They said it was slow growing, decades maybe,
but now, having reached the pons—the bulb
at the base of the brain. . . .
Look, they said, how the brain struggles
in a narrowed, pinched-in space, rummages
for what it can no longer remember:
the old triggers fired off easy as popguns
for ninety years—pump, pump, breathe.

I kneel over the ram's motherless brain
the way I bent over him, holding the hand
that for sixty-two years refused mine,
singing the song he never sang for me.
The crusted mouth. The lolling tongue.
The eyes unable to close
because the brain had forgotten how.
The breath still so sweet.

Snow

Let us speak of love and weather
subtracting nothing.
Let us put your mother and mine
away for a while. Your dying father,
my dead one.
                              Let us watch
from our bedroom window how a slow
falling snow crowns all nakedness in ermine.
Do not look at me yet. Your face is flushed,
your eyes too love-soaked, too blue.
Outside is white on black
and still. The sky, deaf with stillness.

Don't let it frighten you.
Hush. There's time enough for that.
Be content for now to watch the maples
fill with snow, how they spread themselves,
each naked limb making itself accessible.

Visitation Rights

I sit by a ravine dumped with November,
every leaf the color of old pennies. Gingko,
oak, maple, hackberry—no difference.
Back to the dirt factory.

Why isn't that comfort comfort enough?
After all, one makes do: a sycamore
preens in a rag of winter sun and
each mica-studded boulder flinging light away
balls up and waits for heat. Still,
April's promise is midget, parsley on a plate,
compared to this:

High noon and no shadow. December's black-
white, bone-bark schematic
that snow, like Noah's sheet, rushes in to cover,
pretending the sinkhole's not there
or the fallen sparrow broken in a ditch. Look.

The sun's out hunting for his children.
A once-a-week father in a blue car.
A regular Mr. Razzledazzle flashing his brights
on every lake, every puddle, every teaspoon of water
searching for the bodies. *Too late too late*
says my cup of tea. *All the honey's gone.*

Otma Rood

Shackled to that name, by fifteen
she knew the rest the stars dished out
would stack up equal: a mother-in-law
who cooked forty years for the railroad,
raising eight perfect kids to boot. And Joe,
shot dead in the grocery that Friday night
late August, figuring receipts.

Go to Ten Mile Creek. Look there
for what she was, mud-trailing skirts
in her daily crash through woods,
racketing trees with a peeled stick,
mouthing the words she chewed on each day
of her life to suck the bitter out—same as
the creek hid under its breath, lugging rain
to the long brown thirst of the Arkansas.
Even Joe—sweeping, marking tins—knew
how poetry can settle young on a girl
who labeled herself cashed-in ugly
each time she had to write a check.

Take the turnpike east out of Tyler
where Ten Mile still runs cold
past Kissy Rock, then follow on foot
to where it eddies and stalls, twisting
back on itself to lap at the roots
of the giant sycamore, sucking out
the footings, the underpinnings,
not stopping until the whole white body
drops into its mouth at last. Do you see
how the tree leans back and away, pulling
at its roots the way a woman would
who recognizes the unlucky label
of her name on the underside of love
and knows she has to get away, but can't?

Here Otma Rood must have walked
and stopped to lean. And maybe it was here
she saw it. A bird? Who can tell.
A dive of color then a swoop. Or make
it night, late August, when the wild sky,
risking theft, unhinges all its fire.
And she, widow now and womb pregnant
with the only shot at freedom
she would ever have to give a name to——

Juanita. Proxy. Shooting star.

Ghost Story for December

Would it be any comfort to know the dead we love
are looking out from behind thick glass at us.
              —*Eamon Grennan*

In Virginia, snow lasts two days
then melts, leaving doilies on lawns
and lumps of swan on the berm.

A woman shivers in a yellow parka,
carrying her gloves. She walks
looking for signs of her father,
last reported not moving
and aloof in his satin cupboard
waiting for seepage. She needs
to know he'll stay there
through spring rain and the root
inching a rope toward his heart.

Already she's heard the first fly
of next year buzzing her pane, notes
in her journal how grass in Virginia
gets a head start, holding its green
through winter. She worries
what a twitch of warmth can budge
deep in the sift of soil. And if here
spring comes early, what does it mean
for the father buried in Florida
where hibiscus and heliotrope
and red passionflower
lush as pain keep coming coming
as if there were no such thing as death?

Cave hic poetae. Beware of poets
who play with the dead. It's no comfort
to know her father watches

from behind glass. Or rises
to the surface of a lake—dead fish—
repeating her old name *rotten daughter*
rotten daughter through his mouth hole.

The father she wanted was given,
five days before the end. And that
in the form of a baby whose last breath
settled the lid on a gift. Don't open it.

The Sound

Since your death
I remember you as I've written
not how you were. The old forgiveness
of child hand in yours comes through
the pen.

Dandelions dot these woods,
violet, bellwort, little pink things.
Last year's death safely underfoot.
Another spring. Another urge
to reinvent.

But even in April—
the forest rinsed in sun
and empty as a waiting jar—I panic
at certain sounds. Not the woodpecker
typing in his high office

or the rotten limb
banging on her dead mother for heat.
But finer: jitters of birds or
last year's dead leaf still rattling
its umbilical twig.

A dogwood
proselytizes in pink, holds up
his crosses—witness, prophet,
Lazarus of the Snows. But look—
here on the path

two dead moles.
And deer, a double trail
ending suddenly. Their final prints
dug in as if stabbed by a sound,
they stiffened

in moonlight,
and rigid as two boards
were hauled like spare scenery, up
through slots in air. Old Wound—
was it you?

In an Angry Vein

Last night, I dreamed again—
adult potty-chairs and corridors,
cottage cheese and peaches on a tray.
Nothing that shines. Not even language
to pull me out and awake. No metaphor
to wrap my new life in, only a jumble
of paraphernalia and the red button
she pushes and pushes for no one to come.

Yesterday I did her nails,
held each trembling finger to file
and swab, cream with Intensive Care.
The veins bulging across each ache
and knob, down each arthritic knuckle,
weaving a net to hold them. Poor veins.
Mama's veins. Tote bag for bones.
Each cord, bruise-blue and swollen
as a traffic jam or a telephone wire
clogged with voices desperate to get out.

We play a game of cassino. She naps, stirs,
asks again when dinner's served
and where. I push her in her chair,
earning my ticket (my sister says) to heaven.
My sister's wrong.

A little girl holds her breath
for ninety years. The veins labor,
wrestle with their knots. A story, a story.
Little girl needs to dredge up her story.
And I, for the life of me, don't have the heart
to make her ream it out.

The Fall

The carpet tilted like the sea.
And she who never walked on water
tipped, spun, then toppled—

a bundle of sticks,
Pinocchio's old mother
come apart in her strings.

The way I watched
you'd think it was Channel 8,
another trick at the Olympics—

another triple lutz gone wrong,
except she didn't get up
to do it again, smiling stupid

for the judges. No judges.
Only me in the mirror, ticking off
in a ledger how once again

I failed to rescue her in time
the way she taught me,
the way she always taught me

how to love her love her,
little girl imperious or flailing
arthritic in my arms.

Now she sits in a chair.
The slinged arm prophetic as albatross,
heavy as the cast of her 91 years

hanging from both our necks—
her Purple Heart, her Olympic gold.
My alloy dipped in gilt.

Funny how things break down,
like when wires cross in the phone
and the conversation you bargained for—

the one life you sunned
and watered like a petunia—
splits into two.

Today we share an orange.
I strip it with my nail. The navel,
a hard wet knot under the skin.

Old Gray Bird—please,
today let's embrace the augury
of peel, fallen unbroken to the dish.

No more bulletins from the interior,
the study of entrails, the ominous
bawk bawk of the failed bowel.

I know, I know: the fall
that will end it—hip or spine.
Any day now you remind me.

Mother, not to worry.
The short straw you've longed for
is in your hand at last.

One day you will succeed.
I have a talent for failure.
I've been practicing all my life.

From the Daughter Journals

As whales plow through krill,
swifts stream out of their chimney

gleaning a bug breakfast from the air.
An old cardinal knocks a young one

off his wire. A gang of crows swoops in
looking for a morning argument. I sit

by the lake, watching how trees lean
diagonal, tending to their reflections,

wondering if they too are joined—stuck
root to root—as if those look-alikes

towering in the fretful water,
those dead ringers, were their mothers.

By December each leaf loss will be
set down in the surface records

revealing the skeletons of an ancient
tug of war. What's this of whales and krill?

Here is my center post. Here
where the toad freezes and stares,

and the old oak hangs on to her leaves
all winter, running a nursing home for

her daughters death-rattling in her arms.
Oh Mother, forgive me.

I have bad dreams. Everything
seems to know my name, writes me

into its daily movie. I can't seem
to go more gently into your good night.

I'm afraid you are taking me with you.

Footnote

Maybe after
from your bed of "ease at last"

you'll give your child
a something. A tap-tap

tapped by your own hand.
A message, by fair or foul means,

sneaked out through your wrap-
around of roots. And I, eyes up

and straining
under that nipple-rooting tree

the way others stood
under the sacred oak in Dodona,

god-drunk on leaves grown fat
on rain, taken in easy

as mother's milk.
But what exorcist, deliverer

of comfort, dare translate for me
when from your tongue

of sullen silence
perfected in the grave

there comes
a heave of earth, a groan

of roots dragging themselves out,
the branches

huddled inside their writhing
sleeves of gibberish: the leaves

gone mad
with your struggle not to say,

not to tell your child,
pure and simple, she was good enough.

At the Holocaust Museum

December 1999

Like Dante, we too are led
down. The elevator that swooped us up
and spewed us out, leaves us—
clusters of strangers—to the inexorable power
of no way to go but with each other
and the relentless spiral of design.

We shuffle, slow as sludge
in a drain, winding to the bottom.
We gawk, not in disbelief but believing
this has little to do with us—our comfort
in the face of explanations that explain
nothing, the old jackboot footage
of rantings, book burnings, and the car
that waits for us, rattling with ghosts
on its siding, and the glass case
big as Germany, knee-deep in human hair.

We grow quiet. We have crawled
into our eyes. There is nothing
but what we see. And at base bottom,
what's to see but the dredged-up bottom
of ourselves that belongs only to ourselves
and the moving tide of each other.
We crowd in to look. The eye is hungry—
a dog dragging its belly through streets,
sniffing out its own vomit, not getting enough:
the experiments, the ovens, and all their

tattooed histories fidgeting in smoke
that rose like bubbles in a fish tank
to dissipate in air. Fingers pluck
at our sleeves. Gold teeth hiss

in their case. What do they want of us,
we who can give nothing, reduced to nothing
but dumb pupils staring at evidence—
the starved and naked dead, the bulldozers,
the British soldier throwing up in his hand?
We press to the TV monitors, mob in,

fit our bodies together like multiple births
in the womb, wanting the heat of each other,
the terrible softness beneath clothes.
Excuse me, Pardon, and the knot of us
slips a little, loosens to make room.
In the smallest of voices, *Sorry* we say
as if, battered back to three again,
all we have is what Mother said was good.
Pinkie in a dike. Bandaid on a gusher.
But what else do we know to do

at the end of another century that retrospect
will narrow to a slit, if this Holocaust—
this boulder big as Everest—isn't big enough
to change the tide that ran through it?

Seeing It Through

Presto the magician
drops his handkerchief
and amazingly I'm looking down
seventy years. Down
as from the top of a winding stair
vertigoing to the bottom
where the child struggles to mount
crawling on her knees that first step.
And I want to say Wait
I'll come down
carry you up
for I need you here
now that the banister is nearing
its finial and I can see
the rituals of the sky
speeding up through the almost
reachable skylight.

Honey hair and the sunsuit
Mother made from a scrap. Come.
If I hold you high, you can touch
the glass. Let the last contact
be a baby's hand. Why not?
All things come around
replete with rage and rattle.

Trip to Delphi

Lately, I've begun to look
like my father. Dead and gone,
the man has sent his genes ahead
to do his dirty work. Baleful eye
in the bathroom mirror, the curse
of the House. And so I've come
not to the holy city of Byzantium
but to the best I can manage—Delphi,
named for the real thing, Indiana,
home of the Wabash and the professional
choice in swine equipment. Delphi,
where girls grow up to be auxiliaries
shuffling behind the fire truck
in the parade.
                But I remember
the other Delphi—Omphalos of the World—
how twenty years ago I lay on my back
among cypress, the sky opening above me
consenting to be read at last. All columns
up again reaching to touch it. Funny
how the brain works to put things back.
The rubble around me—cracked slabs
and steps where girls once walked
leading the procession, pieces of
pediment and pedestal, each one
white as a Dover Cliff. Oh peerless
dumping ground to hold such trash!
Hunks of marble big as giants' teeth
and strewn about as if the golden cup of
Zeus itself had fallen off its nightstand,
shattering the ineffable bridge.

But what's the bridge between
all that and this Family Dollar store
in Delphi, Indiana, where I've ended up?

This temple consecrated to toothpaste,
batteries, and bargain underwear. Empty
but for me and the thin-lipped guardian of
the till, priestess on a stool, breathing in
the vapors of advanced righteousness. Oh harpy
of the tollgate, agent of the family curse,
do not look at me so. In the twin auguries
of your eyes, double and doubly I am
my father's daughter. Each crumbling face
witness to the other, split in half
and shattered by the bifocal line.

Depression Glass

It must have been October, right after
the annual hanging of the winter drapes
and the ceremonial unrolling of the rug
from its summer sleep behind the sofa.
Gone were the slipcovers, leaving
the upholstery stripped down to warm
arms again, and the little living room
transformed into a mother-hug of all
she labored for—the luxury of bastion
and snug, the thick stability of thick
pile, purchased with how many
on-her-knees hours of scour and rag.
The whir of the sewing machine at night,
and all those stretched nickels.

My sister would say this never happened,
or if it did, it wasn't this way, or if it was,
I never cried, or if I did, how could I—
so young—know what was to cry about.

A room like that, in the Snow White
haven of the dwarves' house, and I
no more than four, rowing a cardboard
box across the rug, its flowered sea
lapping at my hands that were my oars.
When suddenly, there was my father
dancing to the radio or some crazy song
of his own making, flapping his arms
and yawping like a great enchanted
gull of happiness having nothing to do
with me. Or her. And I saw as through
the glass layers of the sea what he'd
been before I came in my little boat

grinding its vast engines of responsibility,
dragging him under, changing him into
someone other than the drowned beloved
I'd be trying to make it up to all my life.

Visiting the Territories

Come, brush the clay
from what's left of your good suit
and lie down here with me.
                        In the splinters
of what you are, in the marrow's residue,
surely there are traces of your bride.
Don't be afraid. Make believe I'm asking
you to dance. You always loved to dance.
Show 'em how it's done in Brooklyn, you'd say,
whirling me out to the ends of your fingers,
pulling me back.
                        Now I'm pulling you
back, not to redraw the lines or rummage
in the ragbag of our *forever after,*
but because I need you. Come.
Our first apartment, a high-rise called
The Dakota, remember? A big joke
for two New York City big shots like us
who couldn't find the Dakotas on a map
if we had to. Birdland, that we knew, Basie,
Embers East, Oscar Peterson, and Dinah un-
dressing the blues in pink. Dizzy, healing
the world with his horn, holding the whole
damn ball in his cheeks. Who'd not reconvene
his dust to remember that?
                        Come. Apt. 4-C.
Five-and-ten-store dishes and all we own—
a mattress, Scrabble, and a window fan
rattling its dark inklings. Maybe if you lay
down next to me the artless bones, I could find
the true history of the Dakotas before the broken
treaties, the Badlands, and what happened next.

The Shoes

This poem is about a bed and a chair,
about a pair of shoes, and a body
I knew better than my own, the husband's
body my body has forgot. Nor would
I recognize or recall—if it walked
in now in those shoes I picked out for him—
the old hollows, the way our flesh must have
waked and curved to each other, how sinews
of his shoulder were attached to carve out
the place I lay my head.
                              This is about
what happens to what you can't remember
because the mind's job is to save your life—
cauterizing, cutting it out. What's gone
is forced to wander the brain looking for
the warm spot, the open-arms spot where it
used to live. Only things remain—a chair,
a pair of empty shoes scurrying down
the neural corridors, scuffing up dust,
dropping echoes like desperate pebbles in
their wake, having nothing but a voiceless
tongue of dried leather, all frenzy and wag.

The Color of Ineffable

Yesterday on my walk, a Polyphemus moth,
dead. All color drained
but for the great dark eyes on her wings.
How could I not bring her home? She was
bleached perfection, the color of faded silk
or a brittle papyrus on which were written
the now unreadable inks and the cocoon's mystery.

The expert says she died of starvation,
having used up all the fat
from her salad days. But he can't explain
her lack of color or why she appeared
in the one spot between sunshine and shade
where I'd be sure to find her.

I keep her on the corner of my desk,
marvel at her six-inch spread, the night-
flying veins bursting like moon rays
from the center post of her body—a wonder,
a week's worth of wonder, for seven days
is all she had. So says Professor Moth,
and he must know. But I like to think
when her allotted time was up,
she in her hour of certitude put aside
all purples and gold, all buzz of sequin
and flutter and whim, and like a queen
facing the wall of inevitable,
laid the white flag of herself down naked:
elect: the devil's parchment, the angel's chalk.

The professor says impossible.
But what does he know about epic queens
or poets in white? And what could he understand
about women and starve?

Alchemy

Bernheim Forest

In fall the forest turns metallic: gold
fading to copper, falling to quiet,
until all that remains
is the scrape of baser metal—the oak
who denies her leaves but holds on
to give them grief. Her brand
of alchemy: gold into iron, daughters
into a rattling sweater of rusty cans
for the wind to snatch at, swiping
with his hook.
               Mother, forgive me.
Three years gone, and I'm still
rattling in the shadow of your death.
Tramping these woods, I find myself
looking for substitutes. When I was young
you used to sing to me, but all signs
of a pebble-murmuring brook have dried up.
Roots too—for you were mine surely—
and see how these roots shrivel in air
dangling over a dry culvert. Now
you look back from this forest mirror,
not what you were but what you became.
A stony thing. And there I am, still pushing
your chair, singing "I'm Just Wild about Harry,"
trying to bring you back. That was always
my trouble, wasn't it? Even now, stuck
on my umbilical twig, rattling the dead for a kiss.

The Price

We were a process
going nowhere, fueled
on poetry and any old thing
to eat. Even in the bathtub, be-
tween slosh and fondle, we were Rich
and Sexton, Hass and *listen to this.*
Oh, but weren't we lovely then?
You were my delirium, my
silver ring, my Mercury, all lithe-
limbed stream and glitter. And I,
young again and too much in love
to be turned into your boulder—
the mote in your eye.

Today, twenty-five years later,
the trees outside my window
once again dandle their darlings,
tossing in the blue air spring's
green adorables, knowing
full well the coming sacrifice,
the shriveling end. And I wonder
if when these trees are gone,
the future will be able to read
the invisible ink ground into
their pulp, pressed into their paper,
saying *After, there was blank.*
Then there was inconsolable.

The Mythological Cod

Soft-finned and waiting,
she feeds under arctic ice
or zigzags down the lacy
edges of Norway. Nereid
of no fat, stretched sleek
up to five, six feet long
cutting through the waters
of the north. *Gadus morhua*.
The Cod. Sensitive eyes,
antifreeze in the blood,
and a cargo of four million
eggs to deliver. A lovesick
bundle of white flakes packed
tight as parachute, tight
as Mae West in a long
green shimmer with amber
leopard spots down the sides,
long white belly and a stripe.
And from her lower jaw, a fleshy
tentacle, a humming dingle-
dangle packed with sensors,
so she'll know you're there.
You warm thing.

                      Just as
Mistress Quickly sensed
the what's what behind
the codpiece—that fancy
bag to hold the bag
Mister Marvelous rides on,
rests on like a pasha. Sack,
reticule, pouch: scrotum.
That pair of maracas,
that holy treasure trove
of Russian dolls.

                      She mates

in spring. The male
bobbing and weaving
then swimming by her side
synchronized to her rhythm,
oblivious to nets or a boat's
bottom-cast of shadow, its cage
of lowered strings. How light
the translucent bones in their
flesh of white leaves. How sweet
the rites of urgency, the rush
to release, Oh Oh, together—
tumble of eggs in a baste
of cloudy milt.
                    I remember
Grandma in the cloud
of her dementia, standing by
the stove, rolling codfish balls
for the soup, bending to hear
the kiss of each dropped splash.
And how it occurred to her then
to fess up about Grandpa. *Done.*
Done as a dead fish.
                    Battered
by tide and curved as a codpiece,
Cape Cod, named for the fish
that once thrived there, still
lifts an arm, cocks a wrist,
beckons like the Lorelei
to the sea, all the while
hooking like a miser's arm
around treasure. So Captain Gosnold
who named it must have thought,
weighing anchor amid a storm
of Cod—the sacred fish
Christ multiplied to feed

the lucky. A Cod in every pot.
Fish & Chips on Sundays. Enough
to walk on, to pave with scales
the royal road back to England.
A kingdom's purse.
                              A man's purse.
The Stradivarius behind his zipper
or tasseled flap. Rose-tipped
shy or knocking the rumba
to get out. Broker in a three-
piece suit, standing too close
in the subway, with a fishy stare.
Wanna ride this deep-sea pole?
Cod. Imperial in a crown of hair
or ashy pale as my father's
when he died.
                    Enough of that.
Did you know, Cod have
white livers and a vibrating
bone inside the head that
lays down like rings in a tree,
layers to remember? The books say
if you make Cod's head chowder,
better cut away the lips
or put a penny in the pot
for luck, there being other ways
to speak.
                    Once upon a time,
before a place to stand stood
on the face of the deep, the sea,
wrapped in its great sheets
of water, rolled over on its back
and had a dream. And the earth
heaved with it, the sky purpling
with blushing. And all the gods

pacing in their dressing rooms
stopped to polish up their lines.
You know this dream—
how the sea in its soggy sleep
rose, streaming with wet,
knocking the four winds off
their pegs to whizz and bang
against the walls of heaven.
And how Death sank to his knees
and shook in the confines
of his silhouette, for under
the racing eyelids of the sea
swelling as if to break and
singing in the hammock of its aching,
Death saw the dream of the turning wheel.
And hurtling from the teeming depths,
an arc of liquid fire—the Cod.

Art & Science

In chemistry, what's severed
looks to latch on to any other
severed thing: orphaned electrons
zizzing in your wires race to embrace,
swirl a DC-do-ing, re-form their rings.
Chemistry likes adherence, every tick
its tock. Split an atom. What a noise!

Then is it not passing strange
when molecules into proteins make
and muster into muscle, teeth, bone, knee,
that when this vast multitude jostling
under skin wakes, it wants to be alone?

What did Greta Garbo have on me?

Outside my window the great poplar
tosses her leaves hand to hand like
so much change as if she were rooted
to a corner waiting for a bus. How antsy
she is for all this autumn fuss to be over.
Who knows but that November rains
whet the appetite for cold: the annual
jettison of gold to stripped-down shudder
and pause. The air holds its breath. Listen.
One red dot on a bare branch, singing.
In here, the violin's one note at a time.

Leonardo's Roses

from Lady with an Ermine
Czartoryski Museum, Krakow

Leonardo was convinced
sperm came down from the brain
through a channel in the spine.
So much for genius. I say
sperm, like any seed, travels up,
makes an explosion in the brain,
leaving a scent of crushed flowers
in the memory. On such a trellis
true love might climb. On such
a shaky stair, many a bad apple
rotten to the core is persuaded
to polish himself up before rising,
sleek and feverish as a column
of mercury in a tube.
                    Mona Lisa,
whose smile is older than the rocks,
she knew. And Cecilia Gallerani,
seventeen and paramour to Sforza
the lecher, usurper, Duke of Milan.
See how she catches the light
full in the face then beams it back
like truth itself. And look
how she holds the ermine—
Sforza's emblem—how she lets it
tread her arm, claws unleashed,
and she not flinching. This is
no inert female sitting pretty
for her picture.
                    She's present,
expectant, listening to someone
over Leonardo's hunched shoulder,
maybe Sforza himself who follows

her scent up and down corridors
in case he needs her, yes,
to check his arithmetic, polish up
his correspondence. Later when
he's pricked to marry someone else,
he'll set her up for life: estate,
gardens, the works. *Cecilia Magnificat.*
But she doesn't know that yet, does she—
stroking his little white weasel,
patting its head?

Vinculum

for Richard

Do not look at me again like that: between us
is too stripped down to the bare wire of what we were.

The look, umbilical—that cord I thought discarded
in some hospital bin fifty years ago come November.

How strange to find it once more between us,
still beating and so palpable we could

cross over and enter into each other again,
seeing our old selves through new, first eyes.

Plucked from a drumroll of autumns, that one
was ours—autumn of my twenty-third year, autumn

of your final fattening, taking up all the room,
worrying the thinning walls. The rope that seethed

from me to you and back again—our two-
way street—and you, little fish, hanging on

past your lease in a time of narrowing dark,
which you can't possibly remember, but do.

And it comes to me: that look must be what *love* is,
which is why we'll not speak of it nor hunt it down

in each other's eyes again, for you're too worldly
to admit, without wincing, what happened happened.

And I, too conscious of my failed attempts
to fire into language what's beyond words, could not

bear it. Which leaves me holding the bag once more
of foolish thoughts. I know, I know, the universe

has neither edge nor center nor crown, but I want
to think that past Andromeda and out beyond

a million swirling disks of unnamed stars, that cord
we knew, that ghost of an eye-beam floating between us,

arcs in space, lit up like the George Washington Bridge
pulsing with traffic, even after both stanchions are gone.

Silent Movie

Bernheim Forest

One afternoon of rain and suddenly
creeks rise, babbling in the forest—
back-up singers for the silence.
A missed cue. It's November now,
the trees, bare. A light piano of chirp
and scurry is more than enough. Trees
make eloquent speech just by how
they stand or lean in graceful habit.
Or in the case of the sycamore, gleam
like polished marble in the sun.

The towering beech, the naked poplar
speak the language of lips and the moss
that covers them. If the trees sleep now
in this storage locker of the cold,
if they seem aloof and alien strange,
it doesn't mean that beneath the bark,
or underground where roots tangle
and hold, they've forgotten their promise
of smolder and juice. Look at them.
Valentino looked like that—waiting, still.

Permanent Press

When I think of that summer, it opens
like a pleat in cloth: lake, tree, out-
blooming itself. What deep delicious
yardage of suffering: the virginal
July we defended, all the while itching
willful and goatish. Five hundred larks
rising from the fields and all I could do
was stare at the scar on your arm—
the gold embroidery I longed to touch.

What difference that time and pharmacology
delivered too late? I loved you then
in the old way of longing. Four wars,
nine recessions, ten presidents: patches.
Each year another July flings her ribboned
hat into the ring, another summer trying to
duplicate ours. Who were we on that park
bench that defies being folded and put away?
Forget it. Are you still alive? The rest is gibberish.

Getting Serious

Today I started looking for my soul.
Yesterday it was my keys. Last week,
my brain which I couldn't find, it being out
looking for me, now that I'm getting so old.

First I thought my soul would have gone
back to Greece where she grew so tall and straight
she thought she was a column. Or back to camp,
being forever twelve and underdeveloped.
Perhaps, being careless, I left her during the '70s
in bed with God knows whom. Or could be
I buried her with my mother—my head not being right—
but that was my heart.

So I went to where I know
I saw her last. Radio City Music Hall.
I'm six, my feet barely brushing the floor,
and the Rockettes start shuffling out, long-
legged and perfect as paper dolls kicking up
down in a wave. One body with seventy-two knees
chugging like pistons going back in a forever mirror,
same as in Coney Island's Fun House or on Mama's can
of Dutch Cleanser. And my heart flexed in me, a sail,
and I swear I saw it flying out of my chest
spiriting away my giddy soul, ears plugged and tied
to the mast: *I can't hear you I can't hear you.*

Watching You in the Mirror

Suppose I stood behind you,
slipped my bare arms under yours
and arced them about, making you
into a four-armed god, all ministering
to your fresh-from-the-shower nakedness—
combing, deodorizing, touching
toothpaste to your brush—while you
concentrated on shaving, twisting
your mouth in that funny way you do.

Would you, compelled
by the light streaming in the window,
raise one foot as if to dance—toes flexed,
heel down—and balancing on one leg,
glow as Shiva did in that ring of fire?

And if I suddenly bit you,
the way I do sometimes, and you
unable to turn, caught in the bas-
relief of the game, how would you
read me? I have played wife
so well for fifteen years. Turban-
wrapped behind you, my name, Surya,
copper-headed daughter of the sun
who, like my father roaring in the ether,
loves to linger over skin, using her teeth
to know you. The gods say death comes only
to those who blink. Gods never blink
or shut their eyes, but shuffle the world,
growing tusks long with knowledge.

Husband, I tell you, there will be no end
to my knowing. In the reflection of my eyes,
you shall never sleep. If necessary, I will
gnaw each mirror you're in, swallowing
it down to keep you awake and inside me.

Genealogy

Yesterday, Kafka's grave. Today,
the old Jewish quarter, cobblestones,
little shops huddled in alleys. Then,
the old cemetery where for five hundred
years, Jews were buried standing up,
space being denied them. You know—
no room at the inn, that old line.
Imagine—shoulder to shoulder, twelve
to a grave, the ranks closing in
close and deep with not a sound
to give away their position. Twelve mutes
face front in a stuck elevator, phalanx
of the well-behaved.
              Then lunch—blinis
and borscht with sour cream and potatoes,
the latest discovery of my too-young husband,
cookie of my age, who tends to tender me
too careful, the way you would a Belgian lace
or any sad curiosity. *You okay?* he asks
then checks the authenticity of my reply
as if checking my temperature,
for we are off to the Pinkas Synagogue
with its lists of the Holocaust dead—
room after room, ceiling to floor,
you'd think the walls would collapse,
there are so many.
              And I wonder what
he's *really* looking for, my sweet Protestant
to whom religion means pitch-in suppers
and learning to be nice. And who am I
to be treasured so, but the one link he has
to Christendom's black hole and this long
chain of names, not of the merely dead,

but of the double dead, the corpseless, visit-
less dead whose names remain the only things left
to teeter on the edge of abstraction.

What enduring hurt still knocking for redress
awoke in him today that makes him bend
to this wall in a borrowed yarmulke,
too blue-eyed, too white-sneakered American,
combing through these endless lists of names? So intent,
you'd think he was looking for his own.

The Waiting Room

To speak of crucial in a life of the merely interesting,
to have a yen for it, a calling you might say,
is to be perpetually involved
in the act of naming. And yet, when I went
to the one place where crucial happened
not once but over and over again,
I gagged on my own silence.

There is ash at Birkenau
under your every step. It hisses in the long
uncut grasses growing out of its mouths.
Nothing but this sibilance is left, this ocean
of wind-tortured tongues. The air
not big enough to hold it.

Never mind sixty years of museums
and memorials, vigils and eternal lights.
Never mind that everything to be said
has been said. I needed to translate.
The singed grass demanded it.

Birkenau means Place of Birches—
the grove in the meadow next to which
Crematorium IV was built and fired up to run
twenty-four hours a day, so busy gassing
and burning there'd be a back-up
waiting to go in.

Imagine the humiliations of the flesh
fumbling to cover up in that waiting room
of white trees, those totems of eyes. Imagine
your mother, her sparse patch. The unopened
pink purse that is your daughter. Then now,
with the wind up and the whipping grasses
wild at your knees, before the dogs come,
hurry write the choke of terror.

On Deck

April in Georgia and the dogwood
droops peevish. Ten in the morning,
95 in the shade, and the pond—
where a friend swears he once saw
a beaver slap his tail—gags on mud.

But weather or not, new shoots
of kudzu inching across the ground
look for a sapling to mount, while
birds, as if demented, keep up
their eggy songs of love. Funny
how wooing goes on no matter what.
Or where. Just yesterday, never
mind the UV rays taking advantage
of peepholes in the ozone, we walked
our flesh outside—me with my droop
and advancing state of crepiness, and he,
formerly known as *sweet young thing*,
bifocaled now and balding. Think old—
Adam and his girl come home
lugging their baggage and their deaths
but still hand-in-hand courageous
despite their once-upon-a-time bitter
dish of apple crumble, only to face
on their return to nakedness
the white oak's shudder and groan,
the April poplar turning away its leaves.
Damn sun suckers! Little Puritans!

Maybe in November, when light's
absence squeezes the day from both ends
and all last-ditch efforts of October's
in-your-face glitterings are flattened underfoot,
those leaves will look back, not on their spring
but on their final frippery, and what smug
joy it was. That defiance. That withering *HA!*

FROM

The View
from Saturn

(2014)

Tracing Back

In the history of reading,
there's many a cracked heart,
lost letter, stopped clock, cut wrist.
Any cursory push through poems
or stories and you could trip
over the drownings
or the heap of crushed
petticoats fluttering on the tracks.

To the bookish, I say *careful*.
What's between two covers
can creep beneath covers.
Any thief worth his prize
knows how seduction works:
ingratiation: the innocent pull
of words, that belly crawl
of language. What do you
think that first slither was
coiling the winesap,
so lovely, our girl was forced
to write it down, there
on the underside of leaves.
Hers, to sneak past the terrible
gates, hidden in the rustle
of her figgy apron: the key
to what she didn't know yet
but would be looking for
in all her troubled incarnations.

How It Is

Late October
and the pitiless drift
begins in earnest. And all
that whispered in the pockets
of summer's green uniform
is shaken out and dumped.

My mimosa knew, for wasn't
that death fingering the leaves
all summer? Yet the tree
plumped its pods, spending
all July squeezing them out,
going about its business, as did
the slash pine and loblolly,
spraying pollen—coating
windows, cars, filling every
idle slit with sperm.

What does life mean
but itself? Ask the sea.
You'll get a wet slap back-
handed across your mouth.
Ask the tiger. I dare you.

And *your* life, with its
tedium of suffering, what
does it mean but what it is?
And mine—balancing
checkbooks and *whomping up*
a mess of vittles as my son
used to say. My son, the funny one,
the always-hungry-for-supper-
and-the-happy-ending-
I-was-never-able-to-give-him one.

Who am I to write the user's manual
for a life, except to say,
Look at trees, dug in and defiant.
Be like the river. Stick out your tongue.

Why not? What's to lose
when what's to lose is everything?

The Night I Saw Saturn

Crossing the Pacific, flying backward
into perpetual night, and all night
one light on in the plane, a young man
beneath, scribbling. I am looking out
the window, the glass prism that shatters
the stars, and we at thirty thousand feet
not flying up but seemingly across
and headed straight toward it—Orpheus
of the night sky—the light that sings.

What is he writing, that man
who can't sleep so doesn't even try,
stuck in an inner section, unable
to indulge in a window reverie, leaning
his head as I do against the glass?

The night I saw Saturn was because
I pleaded. *Before I die I want to see . . .*
and the astronomer complied, there
on the top of Mauna Kea, and me
shivering in all the clothes I had
and hanging on because I couldn't
see my feet, so dark it was as I set
my eye to the metal eyepiece.
Then, true to the pictures in my
schoolbooks or the planetarium's
mockup, only luminous, radiating
more energy into space than received
from the sun. Ah Saturn, grandfather
of Love, what do scientists know
of the light that lights the pearl? Beauty's
absolute, cold white and burning in the sky.

And now, this man, the only light
in the plane, ringed by huddles of sleepers
as if he were guardian of the oblivious
awake for us all. How furiously
he bends to his work. How lovely
the light lingering on the shock of his hair
holds him—incandescent—reflecting in rings.

The Brain

The brain always knows
where you are. A triumvirate
of eyes, ear canals, tiny nerves
in the joints phones in regularly.
I'm biting my cuticles. Over
and out. Practicing the tuba. Or
guess what I'm doing in bed with
all this flesh? The brain knows.
That's why you can pass
the neurologist's test: clap hands
in the dark. They'll find each other.

Using twenty percent of the body's
blood supply, a billion gray cells
should be good for something—
discovering a cure, unearthing
the great gray owl of wisdom, re-
reading Aristotle's *Ethics*, remembering
where I left my keys—something
other than smug in their aerie
this Tuesday afternoon being clever
when I'm standing at the window
watching the hawk's persistent
shadow, circling.

Ars Poetica on Lava

So much depends . . .
       —William Carlos Williams

The night I picked my way
across the lava slicked by rain
in the moonless dark, all past
and future sliced away
like bread. Nothing existed
but the blade of my held breath
and the flashlight probing
the black and roiling rock
for a safe place to place
a sneaker down. One shoe
after the other, disembodied
from the feet they were tied to,
with orders to swing out, land,
grip, and pass me on.

Two hours it took to cross
that stretch of Stygian black,
having no thought but the need
to prevail, upright. Now I know
what it means to balance
a writer's life. Each footfall,
each stopping point, a fulcrum
around which the body teeters
and sways: a high-wire act
demanding concentration—
the chattering mind delivered up
blank as cardboard with a pinhole,
dependent, in the pit-dark, upon one
thin thread of dazzle coming through.

Because You Were Mine

One day in the home, my father
was struck by a bolt of philosophy—
split down the middle to reveal the last
two bits of his reason. Ninety years
in shadow and all at once at the bottom
of the canyon, the Colorado glints in the sun.

Poor Daddy, turning on his last spit,
wearing diapers and gumming peas.

He wheeled his chair in close, knee
to my knee touching, took the hand
last held when I was five.
All barbed wire down between us.
The bloodshot eyes, for once
not racing, not looking for a doorway out,
but locked to mine as if he saw, at last,
the constant known as *daughter*
he'd been looking for.

Now, twenty years later,
I am no closer to understanding
the words he spoke, heavy with import
as a museum plaque: *You know, I loved you,
and I hated you. Because you were mine.*

But I know truth when I hear it,
just as I know I am his masterwork.
No wink of water lily or sunflower in a jar,
but tangled snarls, scribbles and broken lines.
What else could he have done, given the demands
of a blank canvas: that blizzard in the head
he was lost in?

Round and Around

In the old days before
earbuds dumped music
directly into your ear canals,
there was radio. Love songs
bleating from every station—
torch songs, misery songs,
eat-your-heart-out salt songs
rubbed in your every wound.

A girl thing. Fourteen,
and here come the lyric lessons
of you're not good enough.
A lesson as necessary
as your first mascara and
the skin you love to touch.

Boys played ball in the streets.
Girls clung to their radios
and pined. For whom shall we
renounce ourselves, yearn for,
be shamed by, deserted by,
forgive? That is to say—
whom are we doomed to love?

* * *

So I'm dancing. An Irish boy
and he's singing *That's My Desire*
into my hair and holding me too close
for being fourteen and not knowing
what exactly a *rendezvous* is
except to say I want one and everything

else that song's dishing out in the sweet
body of the boy singing it.

* * *

And the music goes 'round and around
Whoa-ho-ho-ho-ho-ho
And it comes out here.

Charlie Greenberg, the redhead
who got caught in ladies' underwear.
His father's business. And the guy
whose name I can't remember—
worked his father's grocery, said
he saw my face among the tins.
Me and Campbell's soup. Peas.
Heinz ketchup. One hot tomato.

So there I am, swaying in Mama's
living room to the latest promise
on the radio. Nineteen and ripe.
Miss Juicy of New York City
dancing my discontent, the way
I will all my life. Even now—

listen to the jazz come out

one hundred and six years old
and still playing Ginger Rogers,
the trees outside wind-dancing
with me. Forget their yearly
baby crop of leaves. Deep-rooted,
trees are stuck in the old days—
shimmying fringes, dipping
and flipping back their heads

like Janis Joplin on a tear
or the single-leg inflatables
in front of the used car lot on Jefferson,
screwed in place but hot-damning it
all day and into the night, being equipped
with hot-air blowers at their feet—
roaring, just like me.

Aunt Nellie's Walk

An oscillating fan. That's
how my Nellie walked.
A metronome on tiny feet—
hips sashaying side to side,
swinging in importance.

Now she sleeps in a chair,
unable to recall how she once
led the Ladies Auxiliary
in the parade and danced
the two-step with flowers
in her hair. Her mind, a blowout
in a bowl. But given a nurse
with biceps and a bully streak
to hoist her up, glue her
to a walker and command, *Walk*—
you'd see it. Even if her feet
couldn't move and she were reduced
to reflex under the cotton gown
tied in back, there—beneath the flesh
trembling to be off the bone at last—
that built-in hint of impudent wag.
Oh Lord, give us back this day
a little butter for our bread.
What shame to have such flaunt
gone from this world. The tap
tap of summer sandals,
the swinging counterpoint
of her arms, the lilting seesaw
of her hips. I swear, that woman's
to-and-fro could hypnotize a watch.
My Aunt Nellie, soul of propriety,
queen of good causes, trailing
in her wake such endearing treason.

The Hands

*After conception everyone spends one half hour
as a single cell.*

Imagine—
smaller than a decimal point and already
ready for long division. Each hand
wanting its own arithmetic to get as far
from the other as possible. The left's
penchant for roses, the right for
the fork.
        Yet how often they search
each other out to wring in despondency,
clap in awe, make mirror images
to cradle a beloved face. How like brothers
smacking each other around, or sisters
picking at each defect.
        Only at night
are they still, the body balling up to be
one again, each part coming home limp
to center. See how the old in their chairs
stare into their laps, each gnarled, papery hand
holding tight to the other the way they did
that first day in kindergarten, knowing something
big was about to happen.

Rock-a-Bye

Not even a smother-mother
holds on to her children
tighter than do these trees,
buttoning each to each twiggy
finger so they'll feel safe,
flipping and flying about—
acrobats in a delirium of green.

I stand at my window
watching the May winds
have their way with these
rooted mothers giving in
to being bullied and tossed,
pantomiming the great
drama of grief and keening
to indulge their progeny, tender
with infancy, their first ride.

We live in a sea of air—
breath moving on the waters
animating all things. See how
the wind lifts the limbs
to reenact the ocean's heave
and swell. How new leaves
flutter about the crowns
like giggles of foam, and all
is up and down, gallop and glide,
carousel horsie and *whee*.

Then my daughter calls.
My own long-stemmed Lilly—
grown from the heart's bulb
and nurtured behind the briars
of vigilance—to say she's found

a lump. What an ugly word
to take over this poem. To squat
on its one-syllable immensity
and not move.

At the Rothko Chapel

Houston, Texas

What is the portrait of Nothing
but the night sky without a star.
An abstraction real as a hit on the head
or a hunk of bread bitten off hungry
with the back teeth.

But if Nothing means absence,
that's another story. Then the portrait
must hint at what beat there, the last thrum
before dying, the last shadow of the last
rope frayed out.

Fourteen black paintings
in a surround with no escape. Fourteen
portraits of the face of Nothing or
of an absence so unbearable, Nothing
saw fit to pour in.

One can't help but want a spit
of yellow or a Pollack drip of red
to latch onto, to say, this being a chapel,
something must eulogize the life's colors
of what mattered.

Outside the entrance, a display
of holy books—your choice to borrow,
take in with you. An amulet to ward off
the emptiness by holding a book
which denies it.

Rothko knew what he was doing.
Sit here and look. Here where the benches
are hard, the floor stone, blocks of stone
trailing footsteps of fading echo
unlike the colors

you strain to see but can't,
being bled out—that Wednesday, right
across both arms. What he said art is:
The simple expression of a complex thought.
Simple. Straight as a razor.

The Runner

Having nothing to think about
but the fact of nothing to think about,
nights like these she lies in bed
staring into the dark. Her mind
running in circles around
that emptiness. Her only alternative—
to chew her rag, that grimy
reconstruction of slights
and wasted days.

Outside the window
the moon mocks.

She gets up, paces, stops
at the loaded bookcase—
old remedy—studies
the configurations of dust,
constellations of dried auguries.
Old tea leaves in a cup.

How deep is this rut she's run?
Deep as gravity. The blank space
she races around congealed into a solid
the way a black hole becomes
the mother you can never get out of.

Three Takes on a Couplet by Neruda

1.

Let us forget with generosity
those who cannot love us,

who would put a grade
on all our sitting downs

and standing ups. Who seek
like a can opener to pry,

to peer inside and catch us
in all our inconsistencies.

What else can one do
in such a case but turn away?

Only the rain is allowed entry.
Only the rain and the lover.

2.

Look at this morning's sky
blotchy with cloud, the sun

trying so hard, falling in splinters
all over the lawn. Lighthouse

that cannot hold its beam together.
If we, the poet says, must forget

those who cannot love us,
how *can* we, given this

splintery light roiling over us
like tide in an underwater drown,

when to forget—generous
or no—means setting the clock ahead

into our own oblivion
which will come soon enough.

3.

First reading, you would think
he meant forgive rather than forget.

But no, his comfort was to forget
and concentrate on what exists

and will go on without us—

the sea, the pines, the *tang*
of sun and salt, where from

the mortuary of the seaweed
rises the smell of birth and decay.

Tell me, Signor Ghost,
what beach did *you* walk

where the waves came in
and backed out without you?

Raised their humps to fall
at your feet before sliding away

leaving a shell, a bit of weedy
remembrance in the sand?

What is the world without us in it?

Where did other people take you
that you forgot that?

The Real Thing

You can always tell the Greek
from the Roman copy, the same
way the lover knows the lover
in a crowded room and how
not to get in the way
or fill the space between
with finger food or chat. To just
let it come—head on and straight—
the real thing.
    I was nineteen,
New York, and he wasn't even
Greek but second-generation
Polish with a wife on vacation.
(How tacky can you get?)
But if he wasn't the real thing,
he was as close as I ever got—
love's seal and stamp, my first
journal entry, my preview
of coming attractions, my
press your head to the X
on the wall—desire.
I still see him walking away
down Eighth Street in the day's
last lingering light. Golden he was.
Even the sun was stuck on him.

All these years, persistent
as a jailhouse dream, he's been
with me—my favorite CD played
on long car trips, or in the tube
of an MRI when the only itch
you're allowed to scratch
is a bite of memory. And when
I finally decided to push delete,

for after all, enough is enough,
I couldn't. So burned in he was—
his left wrist bone, his arm's sun-
kissed treasury of fine gold hairs.

Behind the Door

for R.

Letter left in a pocket, strange
earring in a glove compartment—
such simple things—and the world
implodes. Wife rattling around
a house that used to be home,
child staring at her plate, picking
through her peas. The lover lost
without love's current that had
like a river carried him so long:
the sweet rush he'd lived in—
tent in the woods, motels in
how many towns. And, of course,
the unnamed, the dear someone
somewhere sitting by a phone,
daring it to ring. Do not think
I am a stranger to this story:
the promises, the required apologies,
the ritual baring of the jugular.

Oh friend, be warned. The heart
may not stay in storage long,
riding an iron track, obedient
as a shooting-gallery duck.
A heart wants to be used, fed,
nourished on nuzzle and whim,
practicing the skills it's learned
of whisper and cunning. It needs
to believe that on any ordinary night
before the pitiful throbbing stops
and the body—that new amazing toy—
is laid out and displayed like a plastic
floral arrangement, a rocket
will slip in low under the radar,

roaring and flashing lights: the stars'
own emissary. And why, but to test
the line of *Do Not Cross*, the line
of unprofitable. The heart is not
mollified by notions of safety nor apt
to thrive on a diet of crackers and milk.
It wants what it wants: what's behind
the door, knowing full well the key
swings on a rope hanging from one's
own neck. That's the place, isn't it?
Such sweet skin, there in the neck's
hollow where she'd lay her mouth,
cupping the pulse as if to drink
and hold inside her all that ecstasy,
that mad hammering before it dies away.

Red Camellia

The bush has reaped her reward:
she cannot hold up her arms. A salute
to her location at the corner of the house
where the sun is beguiled to stop all day,
and the wasp tending its cells under
the shed roof swoons at the riot of red
multiplying in its compound eyes.

March has finally given way,
and spring in Georgia, primed
with lascivious plumpings,
has sent word: we've little time.
The camellia has waited all year
locked in her thin verticals
for the sun's first hot speech.
Now she answers—one voice
blowing from two-hundred mouths.

Love, I want to talk camellia talk,
quick, before summer's endless
conscription in a green uniform—
that stifling march into fall.
Speak to me. Be my sun, my day star.
Look into my eyes until I'm lost to sight,
then juice me up red and barbarous:
a phalanx of redcoats, a four-alarm fire.
I'm tired of pork roasts and ease
in an easy chair. Bring me one more
season. A reason. Bring it in your hands.

FROM

Blood Weather

(2019)

Drawing the Triangle

Mathematics can be more exquisite than poetry.
—Yakov Sinai

Outside my window
the hawk reels exquisite,
circling down. Point of view
is all it takes to name a spiral
of death exquisite. To the mouse
running desperate, any hole
under the darkening shadow
would prove the same.
                    But to the hawk
whose chicks wait in the tall pine,
open-beaked and insistent, that mouse—
frozen now and shivering in his velvet,
the beads of his eyes registering
the blank of nowhere to hide—is exquisite.
                    And so geometry
dictates. I watch the hawk, the hawk
the mouse, the mouse (poor thing)
the haven that's not there. It's here.
You're looking at it.

The Interview

You ask who's to blame. Me.
I am to blame. For what?
Maybe the whole business.

You ask where I come from.
If I knew I'd tell you. Could be
I'm still there. But right now

I'm by the river. I go there
looking for four-leaf clovers.
When I find one, I give it away.

If you come, I'll give you
a fresh one for your buttonhole.
What I remember most

about the earth? A pond I saw
late one spring afternoon, algae
inching out from the edges—

a green sludge that by late July
would meet in the middle,
buttoning the pond up for good.

An old sweater. A blind man's
eye. I saw dragonflies too—
jewels flitting over the water

fastened to each other. It seems
nature's way, this buttoning.
And there were creature stirrings

like castanets, and from far away
an elegy of tin flutes. I hope
you will come. I've pressed a few

four-leaf clovers in a book in case
I can't find new ones anymore.
And since you asked, yes, I much

prefer quiet. A hush, a silence.
The marbles of ancient Greece
made vivid speech by gleaming.

Portrait of Poet in Stroller and Awe

Honey-haired and apple-cheeked,
I am four. Bundled up, going store
to store down St. Nicholas. Mother
in her black coat trimmed in fur, hat
cocked over one eye. We are shopping.

Frischling's for farmer cheese and eggs.
The Appetizing Store for sauerkraut
forked up, dripping from the barrel.
Pete's Italian Market where sea bass
and snapper thrash in a too-small vat
before the hit on the head, the icy
bed of one-eye-up laid out like jewels.

But it's the butcher's opening bell
that calls me back. The rack of knives
and polished grinder. Axes and saws.
The shining wand of the sharpener—
its slither sound of steel licking steel.
The ancient writing of the butcher block
streaked with cuts and sacrifice. White apron,
hand-wiped and stiff with a day's red work.
Jelly-globs of liver in a white enameled pan.
Chicken guts pulled out and dumped.
Sawdust on a clean floor and the honest
working hands—blunt-fingered and stained.

No plastic wrap or Styrofoam trays.
Just blood and bone. And Mother—content
only with perfection—flicking a bit of lint
off her sleeve, biting her lip, eyeing the scales.

Deep Purple

Monday, and today's job is cleanup.
I'm humming an old song to keep
me company, something about purple
and a garden wall. The children
are concerned, for it was only yesterday
I measured out my future, stretching
greedy-big as open arms could reach.
Now here I am, backsliding into old lyrics.

I'm reminded of a woman I once knew
who loved purple—not lavender, that sickly
excuse—but deep purple. She wore it,
painted the inside of her house with it,
her lips, her nails, the bottom of her pool
where she'd spend long afternoons floating
in tinted water. She claimed she didn't
know the song, neither words nor tune,
written before her time, but there, behind
her eyes, behind her studied cheerfulness,
it must have existed. Not the doo-wop version
that ruined it, but the old one that a patched-up
woman might have a need for.

I know, this has little to do with cleaning,
except to say her house was spotless,
not a thing out of place, as if she spent
each morning shoving back in a back closet
too deep for any rag to reach, a memory.
I want to think it was about love. About
a cherished someone sucked prematurely
out of this world, draining away like
a slow twilight into the ground. A lingering
subtraction that left her lost, wandering
in deep purple, nightshade, and sorrow.

From the Book of Accounts

I speak of work. How he'd come home
coughing wet and loose in the chest

from the Chesterfields, the hauling
of bundles. How he'd stumble to the sofa—

long underwear drooping at the seat—
flop down, snoring before his head

hit the armrest. Seven o'clock and blotto
as a burnt-out bulb, while across the room

far into the night, Mother and I for her sake
played cards, shuffled and dealt, shuffled

and dealt. So much thin-lipped work
it took to arrange and rearrange

the hand she'd been given. So much
work to have to pick up every morning

the death card of hard labor
that any cut deck eventually lays bare.

All those hours of heavy lifting
to gather, dole out, and try again—

draw and discard, draw and discard
amid grunts from the sofa—troubled dreams

and fortune's shuffle. Night after night,
the long march of deuces and kings,

three of a kind, four of a kind, any kind,
before she'd finally get up to shake his shoulder

and walk him to bed, while I'd wait for her
to come back, sit down, and tally up the points.

Lady Macbeth

If you must, fault her for having
abandoned her own life until it echoed
hollow as the crown he tightened
around her head. But who can separate
the tangled coils of mating bodies?
Having no center, she latched on to his,
using the only art she had—the hiss
of influence. And he, like a snake
lapping yolk from an egg, drained her.

Think of the hours she spent
waiting, hanging on each letter,
bathing herself, creaming herself,
for wasn't he her all in all—
the mouth of him, the sweaty
smell of him, the ropey arms she'd
crawl into, cherished as the crown
she thought she was to him, the him
who swore they'd be together, love-
locked even to the slime pits of hell.
The him to whom she gave her everything—
breasts, belly, hands. Oh, how he'd
fondle her hands, feast on her hands,
undress them slowly, slipping off
each ring, licking each knuckle. Who
was she looking for that terrible
sleepwalking night? An empty
wraith sucked dry and used up.
What was left of her
at the end to wash?

Whose blood was that?

Dumped at Heaven's Gate

When a hurricane spirals
down, spinning like an unhooked
tongue shrieking in the wind's
wet mouth, beheading trees
and cracking open the sky,

pregnant cows in the fields
let down their calves. Whether
the cause is barometric pressure
or the trauma of a bovine nightmare,
the legs buckle and the great spasms
of the uterine walls begin. All day
and into the night, hit by a fury
of flying leaves and limbs
she labors: a fifteen-hundred-
pound bellow nailed to the spot.
All the world's misery concentrated
in that heaving flesh, that drenched
monolith of quiver and rolling eyes.

And if in the wind's howl and rain,
her warm, slick package manages
to slip out and live, and she—
remembering to turn her head and
lick it clean—blinks to find it next morning
wobbling on first legs, that too is Easter.

Mirage

Across Kachemak Bay
black mountains rise like judgment,
towering above the inlet, black
streaked with snow. Black,
white. Nothing in between.

When suddenly like a phantom
floating across the water,
a fishing boat chugs past, and there
we are again, steaming out of Freeport
with Captain Charlie. Little family
bundled up against the cold.

And it must be close to noon
for there's Mother doling out
the egg-salad sandwiches loaded
with lettuce for health and green
good fortune. The bay too, a green
bounty crowned by white flashes
of gulls skimming low over the stern
to eye what the wake churned up.
And look, there at the rail, chumming
for fish, that's my father, roaring
his smutty songs with mother laughing
because they were in the open air
and free to let themselves be—Oh
dare I say it—happy. What difference
if the fluke or flounder weren't biting,
for wasn't it fluke enough their being
at peace for just this once? On the scales
of judgment, shouldn't that day—snatched
from the angry current of the rest—count?
Add up to something? That day when the gulls
weighed in, balancing the light on their wings.

In an August Mirror

Now is the time of ironweed, knotweed,
thistle and heavy heat—simmering and brutal.

Now is the time of no time when all days
rise in the oven the same and go forth in single file.

Ninety-six degrees, a sea of grasses too heat-
stunned to move, and I, standing in their midst—

a foolish woman straining like Odysseus
to hear the sirens sing. When suddenly, there,

from the field's buggy depths of buzz, rustle,
and drone—rubbing legs and scraping wing—

the incessant cry of insatiability, the jittery song
of *last chance*, *last chance*. Each note, a letter

of the earth's alphabet. Each note, another stitch
knit into the scarf. Never mind decorations

of goldenrod and doilies of Queen Anne's lace
or the interminable grasses standing upright

and righteous as a society of burning saints.
I know who I am. I know with whom I belong.

Wasps

Last spring, wasps took over
the bluebird house. Squatters
gnawing out the entryway
for the wood and saliva soup
needed for nests. Good
tenants they were too—
clean, quiet, busy: each egg
nestled in its hexagonal crib,
coverlets tucked and tended to.

When the birds arrived, flashing
their blue entitlement, they took
one look and left. We too stayed clear.
Some goings-on one shouldn't
mess with. Motherhood for instance.

Trouble is, that holy state doesn't
last. Lately my son has fallen
for a 1990 BMW, revving her up
to race her. He's installed a roll
cage, head and neck restraints,
wears flame-retardant gloves
and a Nomex bodysuit lest she
combust and finish him off good.

This is the child whose pajamas
caught fire when he was seven,
the child whose layers of skin
I watched curl back black
from the galloping edge of burning,
the gleaming front line of terror.
And now, just when I need it, my old
mother-song of *Like hell you will*
doesn't work anymore. What pedestal
is left for me to stand on? What

good are eyes in back of the head
without the advantage of clout?

He agrees, his laugh ringing me round
the way it always did: seed of my
November, brown-eyed dearest of boys.

I think I need lessons from the wasps,
for am I not also maker of paper nests,
wrought and tended to? And do I not
also feed on nectar and fallen fruit?
O Queen of buzz and sovereign care,
when does one stop gnawing at the heart's hole—
that entryway, that mother price? That sting.

Metamorphosis

Before she died, my mother
practiced turning herself into stone.
Now she sits—a rock on my father's grave,
six feet above his reach. Each spring
he punches a hole in his roof,
sending up a riot of yellow flowers
to tempt her into softening. The tendrils
of his need claw the air, grope to touch her,
but she will have none of it.

The sun goes up, comes down.
Nothing changes. I've walked this
manicured lawn, its straight and narrow
in a wrap-around of grief long enough.
I've tried to lift her, move her
to where he's not, but she's become
too heavy for my scraped arms to hold.

Maybe after walking this earth for
ninety-five years, she should be allowed
to turn into whatever she wants.
Not just a stone but a boulder
flaunting bulk and weight. A sumo
wrestler of a boulder, bristling
and unyielding. The Rock of Gibraltar—
that frowning monolith born to guard
the Mediterranean's western gate
and blot out the sun. That mother rock,
beyond which—those ancient Greeks said—
you fall off the earth.

All for the Love of You

for Bruce

On the day Daisy just plain
died, Kenneth Haydon of Benton
"left earth to shake hands with Jesus"
and La'Kesha Walker, youngest
of six, "passed through the gates
of Heaven." Whether angels sang
or if there were hugs, backslapping,
or kisses on both cheeks *à la française*,
I don't know, but I tell you,
it was a great day here on Earth
for the Paradise Casket Company,
who recorded record profits from all
that fancy travel going on. But Daisy,
she went sterling, unadulterated, her son
holding her hand and singing her out.
The song, from America's old songbook,
for the oldest love story in the world.
Mother and child. Daisy and son.
Never mind his sixty years and her ninety-four.
Never mind the platitudes about a long life
well lived. It was mother and son
all over again. Michelangelo's *Pietà*
repeated, and if he could, gray hair, PhD
and all, he'd have crawled into the cold marble
of her lap if only to be close to the womb
he'd come from, that day sixty years ago
when the two of them, laboring all night,
rode the high hills of pain, she behind,
he in front, head down and coming,
the way he is now—pedaling hard
into that first cold slap of mourning.

Asking Forgiveness

for Bruce

When we cleaned out Daisy's house,
dragging one hundred and twenty-six
black bags to the curb. When you
packed up the basement and garage
while I opened her top dresser drawer
to fold—*gently gently*—what no
mere daughter-in-law has rights to.
Then suddenly, because how could
she be gone, I saw her hands again
patting her fresh-from-the-beauty-parlor
hair, the same style as in the photos
taken when she was twenty—photos
found in a shoebox stuffed with letters
from her Robert and the war. Photos
you spread out on all the little tables
at the viewing, passing them among
the guests—*see, see what she was*—
while she, in her travel clothes, lay
among us, oblivious for the first and
only time to the choke of your sorrow.
What could I do to save you, having
myself to beg pardon for? I stood
by her box and, sliding my hand in
to finger the white collar of her dress,
asked forgiveness. For I had taken
in my two rough hands the forbidden
of another: the cotton-crotched, the lace-
trimmed, the cupped, the pink and final
nightgown. The delicates worn and warmed
by her, the crushables that clung to her:
her fragile comforts, her son.

Clytemnestra, Unleashed

Lovingly, she poured the scented
water into his bath, helped him off
with his robe, planting little kisses
across his back, then shot the bolt home
and went at him with an axe. His left foot
she grabbed first, then sloshing forward
on her knees, crawled over the fallen
mountain of his body, hacking away.
When the job was done, she stood before
the palace doors, dripping righteous
in the red evidence of her vengeance.

Always the simmering question—
what to do with her life, the endless
waiting for what the oracle promised,
what the stars writ large. One thing
she knew: the jailhouse pacing
on the parapets would stop, the dry
winds from the east that brought no news
would stop. For now at last, the giddy
joy of action: breathing hard, the sticky
handle of the chopper she'll not put down.

Curse by curse, rattle by rattle,
the press of bones piled up behind her,
scraping and jostling for attention.
Time to clean out this house.
Sacrifice for sacrifice, murder for murder.

Her lover hid in the closet. The deed,
he said, being *woman's work*.

Who could blame her?
Even the Grand Coulee Dam—
holding back and filled to choking—

would crack, groan, and yawn open.
It's anger that leaps and rages foaming
through the rift, churning the carcass
of a life into a high, red boil of blood.
Woman's blood. Unclenched, unyielding,
and unbuttoned. You better believe it.

Donatello's Prophet

Museo dell'Opera del Duomo, Firenze

Here stands Habakkuk, plain as a post.
No adornment, no iconography—
book or scroll—to explain himself.
The marble drapery—from a sculptor
who could fold and pleat stone
with the best of them—economical.
The body, ascetic—stringy neck,
sparse of hair. The feet, veiny, size
twelve, not an ounce of fat between them.

But in the bare bulbs of the eyes,
the sculptor has struck a madhouse look,
born from an urgency that leans
the statue forward, burning with
something to say. So realistic that
when finished, Donatello, with one
whack of the chisel, opened the prophet's
mouth, and stepping back and away,
shouted, *Speak, damn you, speak.*

Whether the statue delivered or not
I don't know. Donatello never said.
But I say, *this* Habakkuk's speech
would have spewed out rigid as his
stone dress, chilling as his own
chapter and verse. The marble
tongue, locked in the dark recesses
of his mouth for so long, with nothing
to suck on but censure and woe:

Woe unto him that saith to the wood "Awake,"
To the dumb stone, "Arise!"

Ah Donatello—genius of hammer,
chisel, polish and gleam—were not
those words the flung gauntlet?
The slap in the face? Freshly anointed
in marble dust, birthing tools still hot
in your hands, you'd have stared him down,
triumphant. Was not that frenzy of flying
chips your answer? your vindication?
your ten paces, turn, and shoot?

Judith

The Book would have you believe
she too was touched by God's finger,
virtue stiffening her spine from crown
to heel. Israel's best daughter—paragon
of widowhood—confining herself
for three years and four months
to a back room, praying and fasting,
married now to the needle and the loom.

But when the opportunity came
to get out, she took it. If that meant
butchery on her part, fine. A heartfelt
prayer before and after should take
care of it. Prayer and a little rouge.

When the plan came to her, whole,
as if in a dream, she threw off
her sackcloth, her widow's weeds,
and unlocked the trunks of silks and jewels
stashed in the attic. Silver chains, ankle bells,
and gold, beaten gold to pull in the light
and hold its spotlight to her face—
the face God had given her just for this.

The elders gnawed their knuckles,
twiddled their beards. Holofernes's army
roaring at the gates and not one idea
among them. *A woman, a woman.*
What have we come to? Her eyes,
slit-steel. She clenched her jaw.
They did as she demanded.

How can we say she didn't enjoy it,
knowing she and she alone chose to take

the hilt of history in her own two hands?
Sawing away at the big man's greasy neck,
gambling with her dimpled cleverness
to haul the bloody head home
through enemy lines. To lug it, banging
in its tote against her thigh, oozing
with the sticky evidence of her triumph.

What does a woman feel who gives
herself permission to test the dark depths
of what she is? I see her years later
sitting at her loom, the shuttle
dropped from her hands in an ecstasy
of thought, smirking to remember
how when she returned, covered with
the red juice of slaughter, the elders—
kissing her fingers in all their obsequious
gratitude—couldn't look at her straight
or hide the bloodshot terror in their eyes.

At the Gates

Paris in June and we are in love.
Delacroix, wine, late nights
at the Louvre. *Liberté,*
Égalité, Fraternité. And each
and every morning Camembert
and apricot *confiture* on a hunk
of good French bread—breakfast
in the park. A bench by the lilacs.

The park, *Pour les Enfants*—
a gated, safe place for little ones,
toddlers, chubby-legged preschoolers.
The sign said so.

Vive la France, we thought.

Funny how we never grew tired
watching them—digging in dirt,
spinning in place, or herding ants
with a leaf. The pure concentration
it takes to be two years old: the gravity
of button holes, the trembling lip
and pride of holding fast
to one's own red pail and scoop.

On our last morning we saw
another sign erected in 1945.

1945. The war over. The park
rededicated to *les enfants*
not permitted to enter these gates—
the yellow-starred ones who would
never come back. I see them
clinging to their mothers' skirts,
coveting the swings beyond the iron bars,

the just-their-size merry-go-round,
before *le gendarme* with the frown
and big stick threatens them away.

Add them up. The same ones,
six thousand of them. Babies
ripped from their mothers, howling
in the brutal crush and bedlam
of Drancy—the internment camp
outside Paris, set up and organized
not by Germans but by the French.

Oh, that the tongues of lilac—
those silent witnesses—could speak
a different end to this story.

You, combing hair in the mirror
or engrossed in the evening news.
You, spearing asparagus, anticipating
the meat loaf, the fork shining
like your life, eager and balanced
in your hand. Can you not hear them,
frantic against the gates, whimpering
for their mothers? The big trains
warming on the tracks. What would
you give for your ongoing comfort
to not know what must have been said:

Shh, no crying. Mama's waiting
at the end of this nice train ride.
She'll be standing in front of another
set of gates, oiled to swing wide
and welcome you in. Up you go.

Baring the Inevitable

Empty nests rock in the high trees—
blotches against the sky—
while the forest pantomimes
in the morning sun a merry dying.

Fall comes to Georgia the way
all seasons come to Georgia.
In a rush. No question as to what's
going on. The spider, the scummy
pond, the blood-red oak. They know.
Owls hoot the news to each other
in the half-light of dusk while mice
shiver in their grasses and holes.

Do not let beauty fool you.
Behind the palette of iridescence,
it's murder that marks these days.
Maybe what the forest is rustling
is *Help*, watching the sky flood down
relentless, filling up its vacancies.
I tell you, we are witnessing a battle
for nakedness, a struggle the leaves
already know has been lost. See how
they tear themselves apart, flashing
their wounds as they fall, whispering
remember me, remember me.

Rumba

No one does the rumba the way
those two used to do it—eyes
half closed, the rolling hips speaking
all language necessary, and we
who knew nothing beyond plucking
daisies and pining, stood spellbound,
for there was that dress she wore,
tight with a sheen, plum red, and he,
all slicked-back auburn. Friday night
at the Y with a live band and *It's Romeo*
we'd whisper to each other whenever
he'd walk her onto the floor, making
the gym spark like holy ground,
and we, backing up to form a circle
around them respectfully, and why not,
for weren't we true believers, or would be
in a few years, believers not in them
but in the language beneath the music
bodies are born to speak, the language
that hit me like a brick three years later
at my desk where I hid in the back row
of Italian 102 when the professor
leaning over his lectern began reciting
Italian poetry, maybe Cesare Pavese
or Eugenio Montale, who knows,
for I rarely did homework or as little
as possible, and maybe I was supposed
to be translating as he spoke the lines,
but how could I, watching him bend
to the need in us, his eyes half closed—
an invitation not to be refused—and I
who didn't understand a word found
I could suddenly read not the Italian
which was music but underneath it
to where he led with his mellifluous voice

that to me was the silk wrapping
around the *real* words that wound around
the small of my back like an irresistible arm
leading me onto the floor, and I tell you,
I who scrimped on homework and ended up
with a D, learned then how to move
past the ABC of the box step in order
to follow him and those words all my life.

ACKNOWLEDGMENTS

Poems from the following previously published books are included in this volume:

Reporting from Corinth, 1984, published by Barnwood Press
Inverted Fire, 1997, published by BkMk Press
Zoo, 1999, published by the University of Arkansas Press
The Book of the Rotten Daughter, 2006, published by BkMk Press
Vinculum, 2011, published by Louisiana State University Press
The View from Saturn, 2014, published by Louisiana State University
    Press
Blood Weather, 2019, published by Louisiana State University Press.

"Economics," "The Reckoning," "Clotho," "Snow White: The Mirror," "Snow White: The Prince," "Stumbling on Paradise," "Riding High." From *Reporting from Corinth*. Daleville, Ind.: Barnwood Press, 1984. Reprinted with permission.

"Stars," "Angel Jewell," "Love in the Time of Drought," "Birthday in Autumn," "Invitation to a Minor Poet," "Recovery," "Flight to Australia," "Snake Hill," "On Loving a Younger Man," "Letter to the Children," "Night Drive." From *Inverted Fire*. Kansas City, Mo.: BkMk Press, 1997. Reprinted with permission.

"*In Medias Res*," "Vultures," "Honeymoon," "The Squirrel," "Hunger," "The Longing," "Under Water," "Storage," "Diapers for My Father."

From *Zoo*. Copyright © 1999 by The University of Arkansas Press. Reprinted with the permission of the publisher, www.uapress.com.

"The Dream of the Rotten Daughter," "After Shooting the Barbados Ram," "Snow," "Visitation Rights," "Otma Rood," "Ghost Story for December," "The Sound," "In an Angry Vein," "The Fall," "From the Daughter Journals," "Footnote," "At the Holocaust Museum." From *The Book of the Rotten Daughter*. Kansas City, Mo.: BkMk Press, 2006. Reprinted with permission.

Deepest thanks to the editors of the following publications, in which new poems in this volume first appeared:

Cloudbank: "Sun Struck"

Crazyhorse: "Mother's Secret"

Georgia Review: "Dumb Apple" and "The Peach"

Gettysburg Review: "The George Washington Bridge," "Hygiene," "Insomnia in Moonlight," "On Beauty, White Tie, and the Absolutes," "Reluctant Image," and "Ubiquitous"

Illuminations: "The Reenactment"

Lake Effect: "Of Marriage and the Lunar Eclipse"

Massachusetts Review: "On the Overnight Train"

Missouri Review: "Pathetic Fallacy"

North American Review: "True Stories"

Prairie Schooner: "The Scarf"

Southern Review: "Refraction at Twilight" and "Weighing In."

"On the Overnight Train" won a Pushcart Prize and was reprinted in *Pushcart Prize XLV,* 2021.

"Shopping with Descartes" won first prize in the Public Poetry Contest sponsored by the Houston Public Library and was published in *Wicked Wit: Poems,* Public Poetry Press, 2020.

"Weighing In" was featured on Verse Daily.

"The Peach" was featured on American Life in Poetry.

"Mother's Secret" was reprinted in *Decade: Ten Years of Poetry and Barbecue,* Seizin Press, 2021.

"The Scarf" was reprinted in *Storms of the Inland Sea: Poems of Alzheimer's and Dementia Caregiving,* Shanti Arts, 2022.

Heartfelt thanks to The Bowers House, where many of these poems were written, and to my friends who have stood by me these many years: Roger Pfingston, Patricia Waters, Patricia Clark, Jo McDougall, Marianne Boruch, Dale Kushner, Tina Barr, Marilyn Kallet, Andrea Hollander, Elizabeth Delaney Hoffman, Doug Carlson, Kerry James Evans, Maryfrances Wagner, Laura Newbern, et al. Big thanks to Glen Phillips, my tech wizard, whose genius keeps me on friendly terms with my computer (no small thing). Special thanks to Stephen Corey, who did a herculean job helping me with this manuscript, and whose generous attention and faith in me over these many years I could not have done without. Thanks beyond the reaches of my heart to the late Wendy Barker, whose work and bravery continue to be my inspiration. And thanks to Albert Goldbarth, pen pal and prince of poetry, for his unflagging encouragement and affection. Thanks too to the Milledgeville firemen and the ambulance crew who on December 24, 2021, saved my life so I could finish this book. And, of course, thanks to my children and to my husband, Bruce Gentry, not only my sweet young thing (still) but the love of my life.

Printed in the USA
CPSIA information can be obtained
at www.ICGtesting.com
LVHW041337110224
771539LV00005B/748